1

Cover designed by Scott Pryor, son of the author.
We are indebted to photographer Gabe Popa for the handsome cover photo.

Little Known Places to Explore in California

Alton Pryor

Little Known Places to Explore in California

ISBN: 978-0-692-68201-2

LCCN: 2016905430

Stagecoach Publishing
5360 Campcreek Loop
Roseville, Ca.   95747
stagecoach@surewest.net

Table of Contents

"If opportunity doesn't knock, build a door."
Milton Berle

1

Alameda County

See the USS Hornet

The USS Hornet

The USS Hornet is a self-contained museum on The Hornet, an aircraft carrier, originally named the USS Kearsarge. The Kearsarge was renamed in honor of the USS Hornet that was lost in 1942.

When you visit the USS Hornet, you are stepping back into history. This very ship was there at the forefront of World War II in the Pacific where her combat records are legend.

Many areas of the ship have been restored to the condition and appearance of her service life in 1970.

USS Hornet Museum

The USS Hornet finished her long career in the news when she retrieved the Apollo 11 capsule and the astronauts who were the first humans to walk on the moon.

USS Hornet was commissioned in November 1943, and after three months training, joined the U.S. forces in the Pacific War.

She played a major part in Operation Magic Carpet, bringing troops back to the U.S. Following World War II, she served in the Vietnam War.

The very first Hornet was christened in 1775, and was one of the first two ships in the Continental Navy, along with the Wasp.

To take the museum tour contact the following: 707 W Hornet Ave, Pier 3 Alameda CA 94501 (510)521-8448)

Taste the Spirits at St. George

St. George Spirits was founded in 1982 by George Rupf. It has grown into a diverse operation that makes a range of craft spirits.

It was originally founded as an Eau de Vie distillery. When it first opened it was a barebones production facility with tasting tables jerry-rigged on sawhorses.

It is now a 65-foot hanger with a spectacular tasting room, laboratory, and a collection of copper stills used by the industry.

Eau de Vie is a French expression meaning "water of life". Eau de Vie is brandy made by crushing and fermenting fruit, then distilling that fermented fruit mash. It is generally colorless, bone-dry, and around 80 proof. Eau de vie is served as an aid in digestion at the end of the meal.

St. George spokesmen say the craft distillation movement has grown over the last three decades. "The way we see it, it is not that small or big is better. It's not that new or old is better. Better is better."

With that goal in mind, St. George has dedicated itself to making the best spirits it can. St. George is passionate about distillation in all its forms. This means it does not release a spirit unless it has something new and valid to contribute.

Guided tastings are $15 and designed to help the visitor learn how to approach and appreciate spirits. Each tasting includes a selection of six different spirits, all made onsite.

There are also distillery tours ($20) which offer an extraordinary way to learn about craft distillation and artisanal spirits. This tour gives the visitor a chance to see where the spirits are made and to understand what goes into crafting.

It's located at 2601 Monarch St. Alameda, California. Call (510) 769- 1601.

Tour the Dunsmuir
House and Gardens

Alexander Dunsmuir came to the Bay area in 1878. He built Dunsmuir House in Oakland on a 50-acre piece of land in 1899.

Dunsmuir House

Dunsmuir intended the house to be a wedding gift for his new bride. He didn't get to live in it with her as he fell ill and died while on his honeymoon in New York. His new bride did return to live in the home, but she, too, died in 1901.

I.W. Hellman purchased the estate as a summer home in 1906. The house was remodeled to accommodate Hellman's larger family. They also needed room for their growing acquisitions from their European travels.

Hellman died in 1920, but his wife kept the estate well into the 1950s.

In the early 1960s, the estate was purchased by the City of Oakland. The city intended to use it as a conference center, but this plan failed to materialize.

The property is located at 2960 Peralta Oaks Court, Oakland, CA. 94605. Phone number is (510) 615-5555.

Walk on the Crown Memorial State Beach

From the 1880s until the outbreak of World War II, this 2.5 mile beach was renowned as an amusement center. It was the largest beach in the San Francisco Bay.

Its official name is Crown Memorial State Beach, and is known for its beautiful sands and warm waters. It was often called "Coney Island of the West" and was a popular day trip for Northern California residents.

While the carnival is no longer there, the beautiful beach is back. It is bordered by lawns and picnic grounds. Exhibits of the past are preserved at the park's "Crab Cove".

At one time the beach was seriously eroded by wind and water action, but was restored in 1982 with sand from San Francisco Bay.

Free concerts are offered at Crab Cove. Bring a blanket or a lawn chair. Food and beverages are available for purchase, but man visitors pack their own picnic lunches.

Crab Cove

Crab **Cove** has been connecting people with marine and shoreline life. Visitors can see bay creatures in the 800-gallon aquarium system.

There are stations for different age groups to view microscopic animals.

Crab Cove Information Center is located at 1252 McKay Avenue, Alameda. Call for information: (510) 544-3187.

2

Alpine County

The Alpine Court House

The Alpine courthouse is still in use.

Alpine got its name from its similarity to the alpine region of Europe. It was named at the time it was created in March 1864.

Silver ore was found in several locations in the late 1850s.

Markleeville became the county seat in 1875, a position it holds today. Markleeville was named for Jacob Marklee who settled there in 1861.

The census of 2,000 shows Alpine County had a population of 1,208 people, most of who live in Markleeville. Alpine County is the least populated county in California.

Old Webster School is a one room schoolhouse.

If you really want to get away from the hubbub and bustle of the city, Markleeville and Alpine County is the place to do it.

Visitors might want to check out Old Webster School, a one-room school house, or the Old Log Jail.

Alpine County has endless hiking and backpacking opportunities. The entire county is contained in national forest lands, including the Carson-Iceberg Wilderness Area.

Old Log Jail in Markleeville

There is skiing at Kirkwood Ski Resort, hot springs at Grover Hot Springs State Park, and the Pacific Crest Trail runs right through it.

The Carson Pass Highway

This route passes through both Amador and Alpine counties. It's a steep mountain route that winds down the western slope of the Sierra Nevada, finally crossing over at Carson Pass. It finishes on the eastern side of the Mountain.

A Black-tailed deer buck.

Along the way, the traveler is treated to panoramic vistas of volcanic peaks, cool meadows, mountain lakes, timbered slopes and rocky valleys.

Alpine County has three dozen campgrounds. Developed campgrounds include

Grover Springs, Kit Carson, Sierra Pines RV Park, Snowshoe Springs, Carson River Resort, Indian Creek, Markleeville Creek, Silver Creek, and Turtle Rock Park.

Death Ride

Death Ride is a bicycle competition in the stunning California Alps. It is a super-challenging course that covers five mountain passes.

These include Monitor Pass, both sides of Ebbetts Pass, and the final climb up the east side of Carson Pass, Cyclists finish at Turtle Rock Park, two miles north of Markleeville.

3

Amador County

The Imperial Hotel

The Imperial Hotel

In 1879 the Gold Rush was in full swing and Amador City was a bustling mining town. The Sanguinetti family built a two-story brick and stone building at one end of town. They called it the Italian Hotel.

The ground floor housed a dining room and bar. There were separate entrances so the ladies would not have to go through the bar to get to the dining room.

Today, the hotel has been restored and is now called the Imperial Hotel.

The hotel is within a short drive from many award winning wineries. There is no charge for wine tasting at most wineries.

Historic Gold Mines

The 58-foot Kennedy Mine tailing wheels are a one-of a kind creation.

The Kennedy Mine is open every Saturday, Sunday and Holidays from March through October. Admission is $10 for ages 13 to adult and $6 for youngsters 6 through 12.

The Kennedy Mine is located in the Gold Rush town of Jackson, a historic mining town that should be on every sight-seer's list. Group tours are available.

Daffodil Hill

Daffodil Hill explodes each spring with thousands of blooms. It is located in the tiny gold rush town of Volcano. The town itself is worth exploring.

The town is named for its bowl-shaped valley. It was originally called "Soldiers Gulch". Volcano has one of the longest-running general stores in California.

The Volcano Theater Company, founded in 1854, conducts a full season each year.

Black Chasm Cavern

The Cave offers visitors a wide variety of beautiful stalactites, stalagmites, flowstones, and rare helictite crystals.

A tour takes the visitor over, under and around mammoth rock sculptures that were created more than 100 years ago when gold miners did hydraulic mining, washing away tons of soil to expose the massive rock structures.

Black Chasm Cavern is located at 5350 Moaning Caverns Rd., Vallecito, CA. 95251. Call (866) 762-2837.

Roaring Camp Mining Co.

The visitor gets a true taste of how gold miners lived and worked with a visit to Roaring Camp Mining Company.

Roaring Camp offers visitors an operating gold mine and a chance to mine for their own gold by panning, sluicing, dredging and dry washing.

The water in the Mokelumne River is so clear that one can see tadpoles and fish swimming. There are also waterfalls and natural rock formations. Phone (209) 296-4100.

Scofield's Cowboy Campfire

Ron and Marie Scofield host visitors at their Red Mule Ranch in Fiddletown. Attendees will get a chuck wagon tri tip dinner, cowboy music, poetry and storytelling in an 1880's setting.

Guests arrive at 6 p.m. in plenty of time to see the wagons, art and architecture before dinner, which is served at 6:30.

Call before attending. (209) 296-4519 to reserve seating. Party crashers are not allowed.

4

Butte County

Chico Home and Garden Show

Butte County residents eagerly await the spring and fall Chico Home and Garden Shows. More than 350 exhibitors provide home-owners with idea after idea for home improvement, both inside and out.

The shows are held at the Silver Dollar Fairgrounds. Show promoter Andrew Coolidge pushes hard to have vendors offering a full range of home improvement ideas. The dates vary a bit each year, so check your newspaper.

Johnny Appleseed Days

Johnny Appleseed will tell children a story about his journey.

First held in 1888, Johnny Appleseed Days are held at the fair in the town of Paradise. It is the oldest harvest festival in the state.

Paradise residents and Chamber of Commerce members bake more than 1,000 apple pies. The pies are sold in the Chamber booth as either whole or by the slice. Johnny Appleseed Days is a two-day event.

Chico Air Museum

The Chico Air Museum collects, preserves, and displays aircraft and aviation artifacts, concentrating on the history of flight.

An outdoor museum displays jet and propeller-driven aircraft.

An indoor museum has artifacts and photographs of historic aircraft. The museum has a research library and a gift shop.

The museum is located on the flight line of the Chico Municipal Airport, about five miles north of the City of Chico. For trips and tours, call (530) 345-6468.

The Bidwell Mansion

This three-story, 26-room, Victorian House Museum is a memorial to John and Annie Bidwell. Bidwell was well-known as a pioneer, having led a wagon train to California during the gold rush.

Among the guests that have visited the Bidwell mansion are President Rutherford B. Hayes, General William T. Sherman, Susan B. Anthony, Frances Willard, Governor Leland Stanford, John Muir, and Asa Gray.

When it was built, the Bidwell Mansion featured the most modern plumbing, gas lighting and water systems.

The overall style of the three-story structure is that of an Italian Villa.

The mansion is located at 525 Esplanade, in Chico, California. For information, call (530) 895-6144.

Feather River Fish Hatchery

The fish hatchery is operated by the Department of Fish and Game. To schedule a tour call the Department of Water Resources at (530) 534-2306. It is located at 5 Table Mountain Blvd., Oroville.

Donkey Derby

The annual Donkey Derby is put on by the spoof-minded E Clampus Vitus in the town of Paradise.

The race is said to commemorate the miners' race up the hill to Dogtown to show off their good fortune when they found the 54-pound nugget at Whiskey Flat in April 1859.

During the race, donkey and drover teams compete to get up the hill and through and obstacle course while carrying 54-pound weights.

The race is a part of Gold Nugget Days. To get the dates for the next Gold Nugget Days, contact the Paradise Chamber of Commerce at (530) 877-9356.

California's First Suspension Bridge

California's first suspension bridge was built in 1856 across the Feather River at Bidwell Bar, the site of the county's first gold mining community.

Prior to the construction of Oroville Dam, the bridge was dismantled and relocated to Bidwell Canyon. On the first Saturday in May, the Bidwell Bar Day celebration is held here.

The event features pioneer craft vendors, gold panning, food and entertainment.

The Toll House Museum is open on Saturdays during the summer.

For info, call (530) 538-2219.

Oroville Dam
The Nation's Tallest

At 770-foot-high, the Oroville Dam is the tallest and one of the largest earthen dams in the U.S. Tailings from the gold dredging era made up most of the material used in construction.

A picnic area overlooks the dam and restroom facilities are available.

Lake Oroville, which the dam created, has a surface area of 24 square miles and a shoreline of 167 miles.

For more info, call (530) 534-2306.

5

Calaveras County

Caverns and Caves

There are five caves and caverns to explore in Calaveras County and this doesn't include the gold mines.

Moaning Cavern offers a 165-foot rappel for daring visitors, allowing them to descend into the huge main chamber. It's located at 5350 Moaning Cave Rd., Vallecito, Ca. Call (209) 736-2708.

Angels Camp Museum
And Carriage House

This may be the largest collection of carriages and wagons in the entire nation. Angels Camp museum has more than 30,000 square feet of exhibits on Gold Rush history.

The museum has both indoor and outdoor exhibits, including a doctor's office and a Mark Twain exhibit.

Guided tours are offered daily during open hours. Groups must be a minimum of six people with a maximum of 60 people. Tour reservations must be made two weeks ahead of time.

This museum received the "Best Attraction" award in 2014. The museum is located at 753 Main St., Highway 49, Angels Camp. Phone (209) 736-2963.

Bear Valley Music Festival

In 1967, John Gosling and his wife Margaret were driving through the Sierra Nevada and found themselves in the small town of Bear Valley.

The town was nestled on the southern slope of the Mount Reba ski resort. John conceived on the idea of a music festival.

A year later, the inaugural concert of the Bear Valley Music Festival saw a 38-person orchestra playing out of Bear Valley Lodge's Cathedral Lounge.

Residents opened up their homes to the musicians, meals were served family style in the lodge dining room, and the lounge was packed to the balconies.

From these humble beginnings, the venue has expanded to a circus tent.

In 1985, Carter Nice, then conductor of the Sacramento Symphony, succeeded John Gosling as music director and conductor. Players were attracted from New York, Florida, New Orleans, Indiana, and all over California.

In 2012, Michael Morgan, music director of the Oakland East Bay Symphony succeeded Carter Nice as music director. The festival now approaches its 50 anniversary.

For info, call (209) 813-0554.

Artworks Studio

Featuring decorative functional art pottery and sculpture, hand-blown glass, jewelry and fine art, Artworks Studio is run by Rory and Lisa Gage, a husband-wife team who has been creating for more than 30 years.

It's located at 1906 Vista Del Lago Dr., Valley Springs, California. Call (209) 772-3742.

Black Oak Casino

Black Oak Casino is owned and operated by the Tuolumne Band of Me-Wuk Indians. The casino has 1,200 slot machines, 26 game tables, poker, eight restaurants and bars.

There is a 24-lane bowling center and a kid's arcade.

It is located at 19400 Tuolumne Rd., North (Route E17). Call for information (877) 747-8277.

Calaveras Big Trees State Park

Two groves of magnificent giant sequoias will awe visitors at Calaveras Big Trees State Park. There are campgrounds, picnic areas and miles of hiking, biking, snow shoeing and cross country trails.

The interpretive center includes visual and hands-on exhibits.

The park is located at: 1170 Highway 4, Arnold, California. Call (209) 795-2334.

6

Colusa County

Sacramento Valley Museum

This interesting museum is located in the town of Williams, California. Visitors get a close-up look at California life from mid-19th century to the early 20th century. Located at 1491 E Street, Williams, California.

Williams Soaring Center

Pilots will tailor your flight to your individual preference. Visitors can enjoy a smooth, relaxing aerial tour or a shorter, yet more adventurous ride.

Gliders are released at an altitude of 3,000 feet elevation, giving a scenic view of the entire valley. Rates are offered for both one passenger and two passenger trips. For information, call: (530) 473-5600.

Grand Island Shrine

Sometimes called the "Little Shrine at Sycamore", it was built in 1883. It is significant as a "unique example of folk architecture.

It comes as a bit of surprise to come across a small Gothic structure 100 yards off the highway in the middle of an open barley field.

The shrine was designed and built by Father Michael Wallrath. He hand kilned the bricks. It is the site of the First Mass in Colusa County.

Blake Garden

Blake Garden is a landscape laboratory and public garden in the town of Kensington, California. It is a teaching facility for the Department of Landscape and Environmental Planning at UC Berkeley.

Blake House is the former residence of the President of the University. It is open to the public free of charge during weekdays. It is located at 70 Rincon Road, Kensington, CA.

7

Contra Costa County

Chocolate-Making Workshop

Make your own fancy chocolates.

This class offers visitors the chance to make their own gourmet chocolates under the instruction of master chocolate maker Rachel Dunn. Chocolate workshops run 1 1/2 to 2 hours. For inquiries about workshops, call (925) 798-4321.

The Gardens at Heather Farm

There's a lot to offer at Heather Farms. It's situated in Ignacio Valley and has a majestic view of Mt. Diablo. There are meandering paths full of plants and local wildlife.

Heather Gardens is a certified wildlife habitat.

Call for information: (925) 947-1678.

Black Diamond Mines

Five coal mining towns thrived in the Black Diamond area of Antioch. Nearly four million tons of coal "Black Diamonds" was removed from the deposits.

The five towns in the coal-mining area were: Nortonville, Somersville, Stewartville, West Hartley, and Judsonville

The area is ideal for camping, picnicking and camping. It's located at 5175 Somersville Road, Antioch, CA. Call (510) 544- 2750.

Blackhawk Automotive Museum

A 1924 Hispano-Suiza H6C.

This museum houses 90 classic cars. It also houses a display showcasing the work of the Wheelchair Foundation.

One of the museum's most unusual features is a 1924 Hispano-Suiza H6C with a body paneled with tulipwood.

In 2015, the Blackhawk Museum added a permanent collection of 19th century North American artifacts called "The Spirit of the Old West".

It's located at 3700 Blackhawk Plaza, Danville, CA. Call for information (925) 736-2280.

Las Trampas Wilderness

The park's 5,342 acres offers visitors an expanded trail system that allows hikers and horseback riders to explore remote and wilderness areas.

Hikers are advised to carry plenty of drinking water as the park's water supply is inconsistent.

It's located at 18012 Bollinger Canyon Road, San Ramon, CA. Call: (510)544-3276.

8

Del Norte County

Jedediah Smith Redwoods

The park is sparsely visited as it is inland and has no ocean access. It has quiet and peaceful meadows and abundant wildlife. Summer swimming holes are present and rhododendrons burst with bloom in the spring.

This is an old-growth forest named for the pioneer who was the first white man to explore California's interior.

Ocean World

Visitors descend below the surface of the water to observation windows to view the sea life.

The aquarium consists of tanks holding more than a half-million gallons of water and sea life. Included are sharks, seals, sea lions, rays and wolf eels.

Battery Point Lighthouse

In 1855, the ship "America" burned in the harbor of Crescent City. Three cannons were salvaged from the wreckage and mounted at the harbor's entrance. A second ship accident happened the same year.

Congress then appropriated $15,000 for construction of a lighthouse on the tiny islet that is connected to Battery Point at low tide.

Theophilus Magruder was the first lighthouse keeper. He didn't arrive at the lighthouse until fifteen days after the lighthouse was first lit.

Magruder's salary was $1,000 per year, but it was reduced by 40 percent in 1859 and he resigned a few weeks later.

Trees of Mystery

Paul Bunyan and his blue ox, Babe, guard the entrance to the Trees of Mystery. The statue of Paul is 49 feet tall, and has a 24 foot long ax. His boots are ten foot high.

A forest trail winds its way past Paul, up into a giant, hollow redwood log. And then back to the Mystery Trees shaped like pretzels and DNA strandoids.

The Trees of Mystery are located at 15500 Highway 101 N, Klamath, CA. Call: (707) 482-2251.

9

El Dorado County

Marshall Gold Discovery Park

Sutter's Mill wh ere James Marshall discovered gold.

Here is the site that started California's calamitous Gold Rush in 1848. In the little community of Coloma, James Marshall discovered gold in the tailings of a lumber mill he was building for John Sutter.

The park has replicas of the original sawmill and more than 20 historic buildings.

Living history days are held on the second Saturday of each month from 10 a.m. to 3 p.m. Visitors will see and learn rope making, candle dipping, Dutch oven cooking, sawmill wood working and games from the past. For information, Call: (530) 622-3470.

John Studebaker Wheelbarrow Races

H.L. Hinds blacksmith shop is where John Studebaker built wheelbarrows.

In the 1850s young John Studebaker arrived in Placerville with a wagon train. He came to California to look for gold.

On the wagon train's arrival, a blacksmith named H.L. Hinds walked through the crowd asking if there was a wagon-maker among the immigrants.

Everyone pointed to Studebaker, for he had indeed built the wagon in which he came west.

Studebaker took the job with the Placerville blacksmith and was put to work building wheelbarrows. While young John eventually returned to Ohio to join his brothers in a wagon-making shop, his fame did not leave Placerville.

Each year, at the El Dorado County Fair, a popular event is the Studebaker Wheelbarrow Races.

Historic El Dorado

It was once called Mud Springs, and was a watering hole for livestock. An 1862 census lists the names of 426 inhabitants. These were emigrant gold seekers who camped around the springs.

Mud Springs formed a County Seat Committee in 1854 and entered a contest to designate a permanent location of the county seat. Mud Springs polled 679 of the 685 votes, mostly from Mud Springs and Logtown.

Town fathers determined that the name Mud Springs might deter growth and invite ridicule. The name was changed to El Dorado.

Wakamatsu
Community Farm

Wakamatsu Community Farm

This 272-acre preserve has an 8-acre lake, three ponds, wetlands and the headwaters of Granite and Shingle creeks which flow into the American River near Lotus.

With the help of South Fork Farm and Free Hand Farm, Wakamatsu Community Farm is again focused on farming.

Tours can be scheduled.

Wakamatsu Community Farm is located at 941 Cold Springs Road, Placerville, Ca. Call for information (530) 621-1224.

Gold Bug Mine

This is a real gold mine from the Gold Rush Days. Visitors can explore the Gold Bug Mine and then visit the Mining Museum.

During a self-guided tour of the gold mine, a video will broadcast a gold miner telling about the tools he used to get at the elusive gold.

It's located at 2635 Goldbug Lane, Placerville, Ca. For information, Call: (530) 642-5207.

Whitewater Rafting

The South Fork of the American River is considered a premier rafting river in California and it's one of the most popular rivers in the U.S.

It is located in the heart of the Sierra foothills, The 21-mile South Fork of the American River offers a Class 3 rafting experience with more than 30 rapids

For information call American Whitewater Expeditions, (800) 825-3205.

Gold Panning

Come to Coloma and dip your gold pan in the river that triggered the California Gold Rush.

Several businesses either sell or rent gold panning equipment.

Where do you pan for gold? The possibilities are limited. On private property, you can pan as long as you have the owner's permission.

In Marshall Gold Discovery Park, panning (hands and pan only) is allowed on the northeast shore of the river by the Mt. Murphy Road Bridge (across from the museum.

Bekeart's Gun Shop features trough mining and gold pan rentals.

10

Fresno County

Underground Gardens

Baldassare Forestiere

The Forestiere Underground Gardens are the result of 40 years of labor by Sicilian immigrant Baldassare Forestiere.

Forestiere came to America in 1901 to escape the iron rule of his wealthy father. He wanted to pursue his own dreams.

He patterned his underground world after the ancient catacombs, which he admired as a boy. But unlike the dark catacombs, Forestiere designed well-lit courtyards and grottos, bringing forth radiance and vitality.

Strangely, he put no plans on paper. Each room and passageway originated in Forestiere's mind as he worked. His tools were simple, a pick, a shovel, and a wheelbarrow.

Baldassare chipped and carved the unforgiving hardpan land for 40 years in his spare time. By the time he was 44-years old, he had planted more than 10 acres.

His genius did not stop there. He planted multiple varieties of fruit-bearing plants at different underground levels. Oranges, lemons and grapefruit were all planted on one tree.

Other fruits, including kumquat, loquat, jujube, strawberries, quince and dates could all be picked by simply bending down. His garden is truly an oasis in a modern-day desert of pavement.

The Gardens are now the property of the Ric Forestiere family.

The Forestiere Underground Gardens are located at 5021 Shaw Ave., Fresno, two blocks east of Highway 99. (559) 271-0734.

Shinzen Japanese Garden

Another garden on the Fresno visitor's to-do list is the Shinzen Japanese Garden, at 114 W. Audubon Dr. Fresno.

The Shinzen Friendship Garden of Fresno is located in Woodward Park. The garden was constructed to honor Fresno's sister city, Kochi, Japan.

Constructed in 1975, the garden was opened in 1981. Designers have transformed the flat and dry 'Valley floor with man-made mountains, waterfalls, streams and a lake.

The garden's design accommodates the seasons. In the spring and summer, flowering plum, cherry trees, camellias, irises and magnolias highlight the garden.

In the autumn and winter, a section of the garden is a riot of color. An authentic Japanese tea house is located in the Tea Garden with the spring section. For information, call: (559) 840-1264.

Kearney Mansion Museum

Located seven miles from downtown Fresno is the Kearney Mansion. It was built by M. Theo. Kearney.

The Kearney Mansion

Kearney intended the structure as part of a much larger complex known as Chateau Fresno. It was not intended to be Kearney's main residence.

At the time of his death in 1906, only the residence and servants quarters were completed. Today, the mansion is operated by the Fresno City and County Historical Society as a museum.

The Kearney Museum is located in the 225-acre "Chateau Fresno Park" (now Kennedy Park). The address is 7160 W. Kearney Blvd. For information, call: (559-441-0862.

Legion of Valor Museum

Located at 2425 Fresno Street, just across from the Fresno Water Tower is the "Home of the Legion of Valor".

The Legion of Valor is situated inside the Fresno Veterans Memorial Museum. The Legion of Valor museum houses thousands of items and papers donated by Legion of Honor members and others.

The exhibits tell the story of America's wars as seen by individual soldiers, marines and airmen.

The museum is open from 10 a.m. to 3 p.m. Monday through Saturday. Admission is free. For information, call: (559) 498-0510.

African Adventure

Fresno Chaffee Zoo offers an African Adventure for visitors. It's a 13-acre expansion which features new animal species in naturalistic settings.

The area has been changed to emulate African plains and savannahs. The site has a pride of lions, a herd of African elephants, cheetahs, and white rhinos.

There is also a dine-in restaurant called the Kopje Lodge. Call: (559) 498-5910.

Woodward Park

In 1968, Fresno resident, Ralph Woodward bequeathed much of his estate to the city for a regional park and bird sanctuary.

Bird enthusiasts have an excellent opportunity to view numerous bird species in the park.

The park has an amphitheater that seats up to 2,500 people. There is an authentic Japanese Garden, a fenced dog park, three children's playgrounds, a lake and three small ponds.

The park is located at 7775 Friant Road, Fresno. Call for information, (559) 840-1264.

Blackbeard's Family Fun Center

Some of the attractions here are three 18-hole miniature golf courses, bumper boats, batting cages, paintball, go-carts, and an arcade.

For the kids, Cap'n Kids there is Blackbeard's kiddie ride park. It has eleven rides, including a carousel, Ferris wheel, swinging pirate ship, antique car, and a roller coaster.

It's located at 4055 North Chester, Fresno. For information, call: (559) 292-4554.

11

Glenn County

Thunderhill Raceway Park

Thunderhill Raceway Park is a raceway course seven miles west of Willows on Highway 162.

The course is a series of fast twists and turns and is owned by the San Francisco Region of the Sports Car Club of America (SCCA).

It is the site of the longest automobile race in the United States. The race is held annually during the first weekend in December. It is sanctioned by the National Auto Sport Association (NASA). Phone: (530) 934-5588.

National Wildlife Refuge

**A turkey buzzard perches in the
National Wildlife Refuge.**

This flat expanse of marsh and tules lies in one of the richest agricultural valleys. Seventy years ago our forefathers had the wisdom to begin restoring nearly 11,000 marshy acres.

For information, call: (401) 847-5511.

Willows Museum

Willows Museum

Exhibits include Wintun Native Americans in Glenn County. It also has agricultural displays, information on Daniel Zumwalt and the Railroad, and about Dr. Hugh Glenn, for whom the county is named.

It's located at 336 West Walnut St., Willows, Ca. Call: (530) 934-5644.

Orland Farm Sanctuary

The sanctuary offers free guided tours of the sanctuary to Farm Sanctuary members from 9 a.m. until 4 p.m. During these tours visitors will stroll through the grounds and see the animal enclosures.

No reservations are needed for these self-guided tours. If you are not a sanctuary member, you can become one with a donation of $20 or more.

Located at 19080 Newville Road, Orland, Ca. For information, call (607) 583-2225 ext. 221.

12

Humboldt County

Sequoia Park Zoo

The entire family will enjoy a visit to the Sequoia Park Zoo. Here visitors will see rare and endangered red pandas, and interact with sheep and goats in the contact corral.

Gibbons and spider monkeys will entertain sightseers, who can also stroll among flamingos and mingle with birds in the walk-through aviary.

It's a real educational trip as guests will learn who and what lives in the redwood ecosystem. Unique items will be found in the zoo gift shop. Learn more by contacting (707) 441-4263.

The Redwood Highway

At the southern border of Humboldt County, Richardson's Grove State Park welcomes travelers with an up-close look at the giant, old-growth redwoods.

Highway 101 winds around enormous 10-foot-diameter redwood trunks. Day hiking and exploring and camping among the trees is allowed.

Benbow Inn is a 1920s Tudor-style hotel offering fine dining. A few miles north is the town of Garberville which serves as the gateway to the "Avenue of the Giants". The avenue is a 31-mile scenic drive through the awesome redwoods.

Humboldt Redwoods State Park, known as the crown jewel of the California Parks System, is certainly worth a stop.

Further on is the town of Scotia, which offers a museum of logging history and a fish hatchery.

Carson Mansion

The Carson Mansion is a large Victorian house located in Old Town, Eureka, CA. It is regarded as one of the best executions of American Queen Anne Style architecture.

The Carson Mansion

It is considered by some as "the most grand Victorian home in America".

The Carson Mansion was the home of William Carson, one of Northern California's first lumber barons.

The mansion is privately owned and maintained and not available for public entry. Visitors are welcome to take pictures and view the mansion from the sidewalk.

It is located at 143 M Street, Eureka, Ca.

Ferndale's Victorian Village

Forbes named Ferndale as one of America's "Prettiest Towns". The town is nestled between two redwood forests in a thriving dairy community.

The village has old-fashioned mercantiles, antique stores, art galleries, and specialty shops. Visitors can hear the ring of the blacksmith's hammer and watch fresh candy being dipped by hand.

It is only a five minute drive to California's magnificent undeveloped "Lost Coast".

Patrick's Point State Park

Thirty miles north of Eureka, Patrick's Point State Park sits on a lushly forested promontory beside the Pacific Ocean.

The one-mile park is packed with potential adventures. One can explore the tide pools, hunt for agates, and look at seals, sea lions, and migrating whales.

There's a visitor center with a native plant garden. There are three campgrounds.

It's located at 4150 Patrick's Point Drive, Trinidad, Ca. Call for information: (707) 677-3570.

13

Imperial County

The Old Plank Road

The Old Plank Road

In 1915, San Diego businessmen wanted a road built to Yuma to attract tourists. A detriment to such an enterprise was the massive sand dunes east of the town of Holtville.

To solve this problem, wooden planks were installed on top of the sand and connected together. As the wind-blown sand covered the roads time and again, a horse team was brought in. The planks were lifted, dusted off and replaced.

The original Old Plank road was replaced in 1926 and eventually became Interstate 8. Sections of the Old Plank Road can still be seen as one crosses the sand dunes on Interstate 8.

Anza-Borrego State Park

Situated in the Colorado Desert, the park takes its name from Spanish explorer Juan Bautista de Anza and *Borrego*, the Spanish word for bighorn sheep.

This is the largest state park in California. For information, call: (760) 767-5311.

The Salton Sea

This inland sea is located in both Imperial and Riverside Counties. The surface of the sea is 234 feet below sea level.

The sea was created by a break in the Colorado River. It is now replenished by irrigation runoff from Imperial County farms.

Pioneers Park Museum

The museum houses galleries honoring the different ethnic communities and their history in the settlement of the Imperial Valley.

It also has a place of honor for the local men and women who served in the armed forces.

It's located at 373 East Aten Road, Imperial, Ca. Call (760) 352-1165.

14

Inyo County

The Bristlecone Pine Forest

The Bristlecone Pine Tree

Located high in the White Mountains, the Great Basin Bristlecone Pine trees grow at altitudes of 9,800 to 11,000 feet above sea level.

In the Methuselah Grove is the Methuselah Bristlecone Tree that is estimated to be 4,847 years old. It was considered to be the world's oldest known living non-clonal organism. Then a discovery was made in 2013 of another Bristlecone Pine that is estimated to be 5,065 years old.

The Methuselah Grove Trail starts from the visitor center at 9,846 feet and makes a 4.5 mile loop that includes the side valley of the Methuselah Grove.

The Ancient Bristlecone Pine Forest is open from mid-May through the end of November. For information, call: (760) 873-2500.

Manzanar Detention Center

When the Japanese attacked Pearl Harbor in 1941, Japanese residents in the United States were shuffled off into detention centers. Manzanar, in Inyo County, was one such center.

It was nearly 50 years after the internment of approximately 120,000 Japanese that the U.S. apologized for the injustice.

Sadly, about two-thirds of the Japanese interned at Manzanar were American citizens by birth.

Manzanar is located at 5001 Highway 395 at Independence, California. Visitor information can be had by calling (760) 878-2194.

Lone Pine Film Festival

The Lone Pine Film Festival is an annual event celebrating the hundreds of films and television episodes that used the Alabama Hills as film locations.

The Alabama Hills at Lone Pine was a "western" backdrop for films of the old west. Many old-time famous actors and actresses were filmed at the site. Among them were John Wayne, Gene Autry, Roy Rogers, Bing Crosby and Barbara Stanwyk.

The festival is held annually over the Columbus Day weekend. For information, call: (760) 876-9103.

Mt. Whitney Fish Hatchery

The hatchery is located on an alluvial fan or natural mud flow out of the Sierra and thus is prone to flooding. Such an event happened in 2008, when heavy rains pounded the area that was stripped by fire, damaging the watershed.

The hatchery stocks the lakes in the Eastern Sierra with trout.

The hatchery is open 10 to 3:30. For information, call (707) 876-4128.

World's Toughest Footrace

This is a 135-mile run from the lowest point in Death Valley to the Mt. Whitney portal. If the distance isn't daunting enough, the temperature is, as it reaches as high as 130-degrees Fahrenheit.

The race covers three mountain ranges. There is also a stipulation. The grueling run must be completed in 60 hours.

For information, call: (626) 583-5100.

Laws Railroad Museum

This museum takes one back to the time when a railroad station was at the center of the action in many western towns.

The Bishop Museum and Historical Society has recreated an old-time village around the original 1883 depot and agent's house by moving historic buildings onto the site.

When the railroad shut down its operations, the village of Laws almost disappeared. The village has now been recreated by moving historic buildings from around the Owens Valley.

Admission is by donation. Visiting hours are 10 a.m. to 4 p.m. For information, call (760) 873-5950.

Saline Valley Hot Springs

"The arid Saline Valley is known for its salt, borax and abandoned mines. Three springs, surrounded by palm trees, create a clothing-optional oasis for those who relish a challenging pastime.

The roads are a bit rough to get there, but once there, Saline Valley is a series of gorgeous springs, each with soaking pools.

Located at South Warm Springs Road, Death Valley National Park, Inyo County.

15

Kern County

Colonel Allensworth Park

Col. Allen Allensworth

In 1908, four African-Americans dreamed of having their own black community. They believed a town could be founded, financed and governed by African-Americans and improve the lives of African-Americans.

Such a town was built, 30 miles north of Bakersfield, which was called Allensworth. It was named for Colonel Allen Allensworth who conceived the idea.

For years, the town refused to die. As it deteriorated, The California State Parks Department purchased the land for the Colonel Allensworth State Historic Park.

The park is located 30 miles north of Bakersfield on Highway 99 near the town of Earlimart. Call 1-800-444-7275 for information.

Kern Wildlife Preserve

This wildlife refuge contains 11,300 acres of pristine grasslands and marshes. The endangered Buena Vista Lake shrew, San Joaquin kit fox, and the blunt-nosed lizard are there.

The area is an excellent place for wildlife study, wildflower study, and photography. Wildlife viewing is best from October to March. The preserve offers a 6.5-mile self-guided auto tour daily except on waterfowl hunting days.

To get to the preserve, take Highway 99 north to Highway 155 exit. Turn south on Highway 155/Garces Highway. Travel 19 miles on Garces Highway. The refuge is at the intersection of Corcoran Road and Garces Highway.

For information, call: (661) 725-2767.

Kernville Rubber Duck Race

Rubber ducks ready to float.

This community is located 53 miles from Bakersfield. In August it holds the Rubber Ducky Derby. The event has been going for more than 20 years.

In this race, some 100 rubber ducks charge down the Kern River. For those unfamiliar with the race, 100-specially ordered and weighed rubber ducks are dropped from a bridge into the river.

The ducks float toward the finish line where they are captured by readied nets of volunteer high school students.

First, second and third prizes of $75, $50 and $25 are awarded. Then a new batch of competitors is released.

The cost to enter is $25. There are specialty races which cost $100 to enter. For more information, call: (760) 379-7785 or (760) 379-3667 ext. 15.

The Black Gold Oil Experience

Highlights of the Kern County Museum includes simulated travel under the sea in a diving bell to learn how oil is formed. It's an exploration into oil discovery, recovery and its transformation into many products.

The Kern County Museum is located at 3801 Chester Ave., Bakersfield.

For information call: (661) 437-3334.

Kern County Museum

The Kern County Museum contains more than 50 historic structures and exhibits depicting the history of Kern County.

For the family, the Lori Brock Children's Discovery Center allows children to learn through play.

A favorite is "Kid City", where children can explore professions as bankers, medical professionals, firefighters, and more.

It's located at 3801 Chester Avenue, Bakersfield. For information, call 661-437-3330.

16

Kings County

Central Valley Pizza Festival

California has all kinds of festivals, but it's the town of Lemoore that has a Pizza Festival. The event has food booths, craft vendors, and music in the park.

On Saturday is a pizza decorating contest. There is a pizza relay race for kids.

The event is held at 350 Bush Street. For more information, call: (559) 924-6401.

Kings County Homecoming Celebration

Kings County Homecoming is a weeklong series of events, celebrating the pioneer spirit of those who first came to the San Joaquin Valley and settled in Kings County.

The event is held the week following Mother's Day. It is held in Hanford.

The event kicks off with a "Roundup Breakfast" on the Monday following Mother's Day. Homecoming royalty will be recognized at this breakfast.

The week's activities will be culminated in the park. Additional activities are held in the communities of Avenal, Corcoran and Lemoore.

Kings County Courthouse

A view of the Old King's County Courthouse.

The King's County Courthouse was built in 1896. It served as the county's courthouse until 1976 when it was replaced by a new building.

The old courthouse is now used for small shops and restaurants.

Kings River Expeditions

Rafters can select either a one-day or a two-day trip at Kings River Expeditions. The Kings River is considered a Class 3 river, perfect for both beginners and intermediate rafters.

King River Expeditions was the first to offer whitewater rafting on the Kings River in 1972.

Base camp for King River Expositions is at Twin Pines Camp. Call for information (800) 846-3674.

17

Lake County

Clear Lake

Archaeologists claim Clear Lake has been occupied by Native Americans for 11,000 years. Evidence of this has been found at nearby Borax Lake and on Rattlesnake Island.

Eyes of the Wild

These are customized boat tours for the entire family to view Clear Lake's scenic and diverse wildlife. Tourists will see osprey, herons, grebes, pelicans, cormorants and bald eagles.

Visitors will want to bring their field glasses. Clear Lake has more than 300 species of birds. For Information, call (707) 262-2401.

Historic Courthouse in Lakeport

Lake County Historic Courthouse at Lakeport.

This brick courthouse was built in 1871. It was the first courthouse in California to be placed on the National Register of Historic Places.

Famous Gold Rush and socialite Lillie Langtry received her divorce in this courtroom.

Joe Waite Gun Room

The Joe Waite Gun Room is a fine display of derringers, pistols and rifles. Notable specimens include "Old Fremont", a Kentucky Long Rifle used by Colonel Brice Martin in the Revolutionary War. There is also a "Pepper Box Six Shot" barrel revolver, a Manton 44 caliber flintlock pocket pistol and rifles with bores from 410 to 10 gauges.

Gun enthusiasts will also be interested in a 60 caliber black powder charge single bolt action rifle from 1842.

.

18

Lassen County

Wild Horse Corrals

Wild Horses waiting for adoption.

This facility covers 80 acres and at maximum capacity can hold more than 1,000 horses.

Some of the wild horses in this region trace their ancestry back to horses used by the U.S. Cavalry and then turned loose on the range.

Volunteers with Bureau of Land Management's wild horse and burro program take part in an annual reenactment of the crossing of the Old California Trail.

This was an arduous stretch of trail where it's estimated one human, one horse, mule or an ox was buried along the way. For information, call: (530) 257-9456.

The Biz Johnson Trail

Paul Bunyan and his Blue Ox, Babe.

The Biz Johnson trail head is at the old Railroad Depot in Susanville, which is 90 miles north of Reno and 90 miles east of Red Bluff.

The trail winds through the rugged Susan River Canyon. It crosses the river 12 times on bridges and trestles and passes through two tunnels.

It follows existing roads an additional 4.5 miles into the town of Westwood. There stands a 25-foot carved statue of the famed woodsman, Paul Bunyan, and his famed blue ox, Babe.

Roop's Fort

Roop's Fort (Fort Defiance)

The Fort was a log trading post erected in 1854 by Isaac Roop. The early settlers believed they lived too far east to be in California, so they formed the State of Nataqua.

Nataqua is a Native American word meaning "woman" or "wife". Isaac Roop was elected to be the Territorial Governor of Nataqua.

There were many conflicts about Nataqua and its border. In 1863, a border dispute known

94

as the "Sagebrush War" erupted between California and Nevada. The Fort played a major role in this conflict.

The conflict was resolved when the California-Nevada line was run northward from Lake Tahoe, east of Honey Lake Valley.

Eagle Lake

Eagle Lake is the second-largest natural lake in California. A natural lake is not a reservoir created by the construction of a dam.

Eagle Lake is home to the native Eagle Lake Trout.

19

Los Angeles County

The Getty Center

There are two branches of the J. Paul Getty Museum, The Getty Center in Brentwood and the Getty Villa in Pacific Palisades.

The Getty museum is dedicated to the study of the arts and cultures of ancient Greece, Rome, and Etruria.

The Getty Center is located at 1200 Getty Center Drive, Los Angeles. Call (310) 440-7330.

The Griffith Observatory

The Griffith Observatory offers a number of free programs each day that should interest the entire family. There are some events that have a fee, however.

Free telescopes are available each evening the Observatory is open and the skies are clear.

California Science Center

Here, you can see the most significant find of the last century, "The Dead Sea Scrolls". This may be a limited time exhibit.

Visitors can also see the *Space Shuttle Endeavor*, one of the most advanced transportation systems ever created.

The museum includes more than 100 hands-on exhibits. It's located at 700 Exposition Park Drive, Los Angeles.

Call for information, (323) 724-3623.

The Chandelier Tree

A stately sycamore along West Silver Lake Drive holds 30 vintage chandeliers that are strung among its branches.

Adam Tenenbaum salvaged the chandeliers from a set-building job, rewired and weather-proofed them, and hoisted them into the tree with the help of his aerialist roommate, Brion Topolski.

"Everyone went nuts," Adam said. "The neighbors loved it."

Adam has placed the fixtures among gaps where leaves catch light from scores of 25-watt bulbs.

Marriage proposals and wedding photo shoots are commonly held beneath the tree.

The Venice Beach Boardwalk

A trip to Los Angeles shouldn't be made without a visit to world-famous Venice Beach Boardwalk.

On the west side of the boardwalk are hundreds of street vendors and performers. Visitors will see everything from break-dancing to broken-glass walking.

Unique arts and crafts, odds and ends, and one of kind items are obtainable here. For the person into T-Shirts there is something for everybody.

Venice Beach is located at Venice, California. For info, call: (310) 396-6764.

Rodeo Drive

If you're in a shopping mood, be sure to bring your pocket book with you if you visit Rodeo Drive. This is where the well-to-do, movie stars and Royalty go to shop.

The short, curving street is paved with Old World cobblestones and features two and three story facades.

The Drive is located at the northeast corner of Wilshire and Rodeo.

La Brea Tar Pits

The La Brea tar pits contain the richest, best-preserved fossils of Pleistocene vertebrates. There are 59 species of mammal and more than 135 species of birds there.

The first mammals found in the tar pits were believed to be cattle which had submerged into the tar. Closer examination showed that many of the animal species included horses, camels, mammoths and mastodons.

La Brea tar pits are located at 5801 Wilshire Blvd., Los Angeles. Call: (323) 857-6300.

20

Madera County

The Madera Wine Trail

The Madera Wine Trail is comprised of several family-owned wineries producing high quality, award-winning wines.

Participants with a ticket can start the trail at any participating winery. At a winery, the visitor will receive a passport wine glass and wristband good for wine tasting all weekend on each of the two days of the event.

For information, call (800) 613-0709.

Bass Lake

Sunset Magazine called Bass Lake one of "The West's Best Lakes". Besides being the host of water activities, Bass Lake is surrounded by Sierra National Forest.

Bass Lake is the home of Golden Eagles
and wildlife abounds in the forest area around
the lake. Bass Lake is located one hour north of
Fresno and seventeen miles from the Southern
Gate of Yosemite National Park. For info, call:
(559) 642-3676.

Children's Museum of the Sierra

This is a discovery museum for ages 2-12
and their families. The Museum averages 1,000
visitors monthly. The children's museum was
founded in1995 by a group of parents and individuals interested in bringing specialized programs to young people,
Tours are available Tuesday through Saturday. We're closed Sunday and Monday.
The museum is at 49269 Golden Oak Street.
Call for information: (569) 658-5656.

Minaret Lake

Access to Minaret Lake is via the overlap-
ping Pacific Crest Trail and John Muir trails
from the Devil's Postpile trail.
The visitor will see lots of waterfalls, wild-
flowers, and great mountain peaks.
For reservations and wilderness permit information call (760) 924-5500.

101

21

Marin County

Point Reyes Seashore

Each Point Reyes National Seashore hike-in campground has a vault toilet and a water faucet. While the water is usually potable, it is suggested visitors bring some means of treating the water in case the campground's water treatment system fails.

Each campground has a picnic table, a food storage locker, and a charcoal grill. Call (877) 444-6777.

Art Works Downtown

This is a non-profit art center in a 40,000 square foot historic building in the heart of downtown San Rafael.

There are four art galleries and 28 studios with artists at work. A jeweler's guild, a crafts guild, a frame store, a ceramic center, a clothing store and more can be found at Artworks Downtown.

It is located at 1337 Fourth Street, San Rafael. Call (415) 451-8119.

Fallkirk Cultural Center

Fallkirk Cultural Center

Fallkirk is an 1888 Queen Anne-style Victorian building. It is the former home of shipping magnate Robert Dollar.

The 17-room mansion was purchased by the San Rafael community in 1874. It is surrounded by 11 acres of formal grounds, a natural wooded hillside, a sculpture garden and a restored green house.

Fallkirk exhibits contemporary art in the upstairs galleries and holds seasonal public events. Admission is free.

It is located at 1408 Mission Ave. Call (415) 485-3328.

Sausalito Artists

Sausalito Artists is a large group of local artists that offers studio tours. During a tour, guests will meet artists in their working studios and observe them in the creative process.

Tours last two to three hours. Call (415) 706-5051.

Marin Art and Garden Center

Marin Art and Garden Center is on 11-wooded acres. It includes a butterfly habitat garden, a basketry garden, and a rose garden with over 200 varieties.

The Center's aim is to promote education, enjoyment and inspiration for gardeners of all ages.

The Center is a good place to share a picnic or hold a wedding. It is located at 30 Sir Francis Drake Boulevard, Ross, Ca. Call (415) 454-1301.

Muir Woods
National Monument

Muir Woods

Twelve miles north of Golden Gate Bridge grows an ancient coast redwood forest named Muir Woods. Here, visitors will find 1,000-year-old giant redwood trees that tower 260 feet into the sky.

Hiking trails meander through the forest and bird watching and nature walks are favorite activities. Admission is $7 for adults. Children under 15 are free.

Call (415) 388-2596.

Ring Mountain
Open Space Preserve

Located at the top of the Tiburon Peninsula is the Ring Mountain Open Space Preserve. This rock-strewn site is a mélange, resulting from dramatic earth movements.

Rocks such as blue and green schist, together with an abundant serpentine, create soils which are toxic to most plant life.

Scientists are attempting to preserve a number of endangered species that will grow there. This includes the Tiburon Mariposa Lily, which is found nowhere else on earth.

Hikers to the Ring Mountain preserve will be rewarded with spectacular views of San Francisco and the entire Bay Area.

For information, Call: (415) 499-6387.

Romburg Tiburon Center
For Environmental Studies

This is the center for San Francisco State University's marine and estuarine research. It is a 36-acre parcel situated at the outside of the town of Tiburon.

It is a setting for meetings, retreats and conferences only twenty minutes from downtown San Francisco.

It is located at 3152 Paradise Drive, Tiburon, California. On site is the Ohrenschall Guest House, with seven individual rooms for short-term lodging. Call (416) 338-3543.

22

Mariposa County

California State Mining
And Mineral Museum

California Mining and Minerals Museum

John Fremont found the rich Mariposa gold vein on his ranch and opened the first stamp mill in California to extract and crush the gold.

California State Mining and Mineral Museum is located on what was once Fremont's property. It has a large collection of mining artifacts.

The collection began back in 1880 and contains more than 13,000 objects. The collection was moved to Mariposa in 1983 after residing in San Francisco for more than 100 years.

Included in the display is the Fricot Nugget, a rare specimen of crystalized gold discovered on the American River in 1864.

For information, Call: (209) 742-7625.

Mariposa Museum And History Center

The Mariposa area was named by a Spanish priest. While exploring central California, he came upon a creek laced with thousands of yellow butterflies. He named the area Mariposa, the Spanish word for butterfly.

Mariposa Stage Line

Take a tour through a side of Mariposa that is rarely seen. You will travel in a covered wagon pulled by two draft horses.

Your driver will take you back in time to an 1849 Gold Rush scene.

There is no age limit and no limit on abilities. If you can get on the wagon (even with help) you can ride.

Call for information: (209) 736-7095.

Zipline Tour

The ziplines at the Yosemite Ziplines and Adventure Ranch are not for the faint-hearted. Those who feel up to the tour will be given a two-hour, six-stage guide-led tour.

Groups of eight to ten are geared up in helmets and harnesses, then driven up the mountain.

Yosemite Ziplines and Adventure Ranch is located at 4808 Highway 140, Mariposa, Ca. To book a tour, call (209) 742-4844.

Mariposa County Courthouse

The Mariposa County Courthouse is the oldest courthouse in California. It is also the oldest one west of the Rocky Mountains that is still used.

Colonel John Fremont argued his case for ownership of the Mexican land grant Rancho las Mariposas in this courthouse. He won.

The courthouse is located at 5088 Bullion St. Mariposa, Ca. Call for information: (209) 966-2055.

23

Mendocino County

Point Arena Lighthouse

Known by early explorers as *Punta Barro de Arena* (Spanish for Sand Bar Point), the point on which the lighthouse stands is now Point Arena.

Work on the lighthouse began in 1869. The Point itself is a narrow peninsula forming a plateau from two-hundred to three-hundred-feet in width.

Three kilns were burned near the point to fire roughly 500,000 bricks needed to build the lighthouse. An additional 114,000 bricks of superior quality were shipped from San Francisco for use on the outside courses of the tower.

A fixed Fresnel lens was installed in the lantern room to produce a light at a height of 150 feet above the ocean. A two-and-a-half story brick dwelling was built to house four keepers and their families.

Point Arena Lighthouse became the first of three tall coastal towers in California to commence service in the 1870s.

The lighthouse is located at 45500 Lighthouse Road, Point Arena, CA. Call (707) 882-2809.

The Skunk Train

The Skunk Train will take you through 40 miles of majestic redwood forests, scenic mountain meadows and over 30 train trestles.

The restored rail cars are reminiscent of the cars used in the 1800s. The train leaves Fort Bragg and travels along Pudding Creek estuary.

In the estuary are blue herons, egrets, osprey, ducks and an occasional lounging turtle.

The Skunk Train winds its way along the
Noyo River, zigzagging through the redwoods.
For details and tickets call (707) 964-6371.

Mendocino Coast
Botanical Gardens

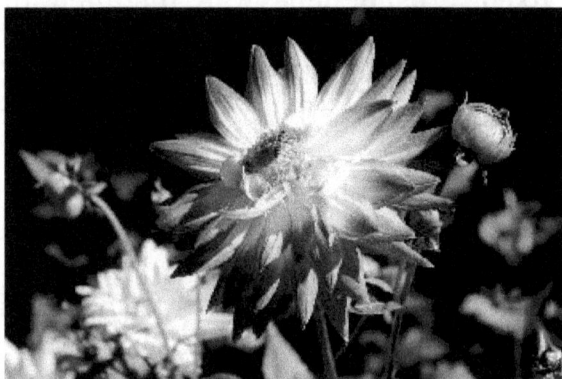

The Dahlia Garden is spectacular.

The Mendocino Coast Botanical Gardens
were founded in 1961 by Ernest and Betty
Schoefer. Ernest was a retired nurseryman.
The Mendocino Coast Recreation and Park District bought the property in 1992 and turned it
into a non-profit enterprise.

Perhaps the most amazing section to see is
the Dahlia Garden in August, when the dozens
of varieties are in full bloom.

Access to the gardens is on Highway One,
about one Mile south of Fort Bragg and seven
miles north of Mendocino.

Bloom schedule is as follows:

- February, March and April: Camellias, early Rhododendrons, Daffodils, Magnolias, Flowering Plums, Pacific Coast Iris.

- May, June and July: Peak Rhododendrons, Perennials, Foxgloves, Heritage Roses, Cactus Garden, Lilies, and Summer Heather.

- August, September, October: peak perennials, Dahlias and butterflies, Fuchsias, Heritage Roses, Heathers.

- November, December and January: Japanese Maples, late Perennials, Winter Heathers and mushrooms.

The Pigmy Forest Trail

The Pigmy Forest Trail at Van Damme State Park showcases low, stunted trees and shrubs caused by complex ecological conditions.

The poor fertility and wetness of the soil restricts the growth of vegetation and induces dwarf conditions in many plants. Some of these trees may be 100 years old or older.

Mature cone-bearing Cyprus and pine trees stand six inches to eight feet tall.

They are able to survive in this soil but they do not prosper here.

The Pygmy Forest can be accessed from Highway 1 in Little River. For more information, call (707) 937-4916.

Glass Beach

It's not just an occasional piece of glass as you stroll along, these coves are covered with sea glass. The easily accessed coves have less than others.

Some believe that sea glass is "Mermaid Tears". It's rumored that every time a sailor is lost at sea, the Mermaids cry, and the sea glass is their tears washing up on shore.

Sea glass is the weathering, tumbling, and aging in sand and saltwater that gives real sea glass its unique frosted appearance and soft texture.

Sea glass may come in many colors, including "Sapphires" (blue glass), "Rubies" (red glass) and "Gem" (pinks, lavenders, purple, lime green and other rare shades.

Take Highway 1 to Fort Bragg and turn West on Elm. Go to the ocean and park in the lot.

Confusion Hill

Here, the visitor will find a variety of fun and crazy things to do.

There is the Mountain Train Ride that takes visitors on a 30-minute trip through second and third-growth redwoods. Travel is on 1 1/4 miles of 20-gauge track. The rider will see an interesting collection of historical logging equipment as the train loops around the top of the hill.

Then there is the "Gravity House". Your body will defy the laws of nature. Gravity seems to be confused and you will be too.

The Redwood Shoehouse was used as a float in a parade in1947. It has found a home at Confusion Park.

Located at 75001 N. Highway 1 at Piercy, California. Call (707) 926-6456.

Temple of Kwan Tai

Like the Greeks and Romans, the Chinese Taoist erected temples to various divinities. In Mendocino, they dedicated their place of worship to the Chinese god of war.

The temple has served what was once a large population of Chinese immigrants who worked in the lumber industry in Mendocino.

Temple of Kwan Tai continues to be used as both a house of worship and to educate visitors about the history of Chinese Americans.

It is one of the oldest continuously used Chinese temples in California. It is the only remaining joss house on the northern California coast.

24

Merced County

The Milliken Museum

The museum has artifacts from the Native Americans who settled in the valley. There is an extensive collection on Henry Miller, half of the Miller and Lux cattle empire barons.

Ralph Leroy Milliken was a local farmer, a mail carrier, and a historian. He started the museum's collection in 1954 with documents, artifacts and oral histories.

Don't overlook the Woolgrowers Basque Restaurant which has been opened for 120 years.

The Milliken Museum is located between 7th and 9th streets, Los Banos. For information, call: (209) 826-5505.

Merced National Wildlife Refuge

Merced National Wildlife Refuge covers 10,262 acres of wetlands, grasslands and vernal pools.

The original idea of the refuge's proposer was to attract wintering waterfowl away from adjacent farmland where they were doing heavy crop damage.

The refuge is host to the largest wintering populations of lesser sandhill cranes and Ross's geese within the Pacific Flyway.

Each autumn over 20,000 cranes and 60,000 arctic nesting geese end their migrations from Alaska and Canada here. The birds will spend six months at the Merced refuge.

Merced County Courthouse Museum

The museum houses 8,500 square feet of exhibits, both permanent and rotating. The museum is located in the county's three-story courthouse, which was built in 1875.

The museum is staffed by volunteers who devote their time to preserving the history of Merced County.

"The museum is located at 21st and E streets. It is open, free of charge, Wednesday through Sunday. For information, call (209) 723-2401.

Castle Air Museum

The museum began with one aircraft, the Boeing B-17 Flying Fortress. Today, it has grown to encompass 49 aircraft, ranging from pre-World War II to today's high performance jet aircraft.

The museum is dedicated to preserving military aviation heritage for future generations.

Castle Air Museum is located at 5050 Santa Fe Drive, Atwater, California. Call for information at (209) 723-2178.

Merced Courthouse Museum

The county courthouse was designed in 1875 by State Capitol Architect Albert A. Bennett.

In addition to its temporary exhibits, the museum's permanent collection includes a blacksmith shop and a turn of the century schoolhouse.

It's located at 21st and N streets. For information, call; (209) 723-2401.

Merced Agricultural Museum

An old iron-wheeled tractor.

The museum features antique farming equipment, gas engines and household appliances.

The grounds have a working blacksmith shop and a model of the New Yosemite Valley Railroad.

Tours are available. The museum is located at 1199 Motel Drive, Merced, Ca. For information, call: (209) 722-2726.

Applegate Park and Zoo

Visitors will see native wild animals, and the kids can head to the Kiddyland amusement park for a train ride around the park's 23 acres.

The park also has picnic tables and a rose garden. It's located at 26th and R streets. For information, call: (209) 385-6840.

25

Modoc County

South Warner Mountain Wilderness

This wilderness has more than 70,000 acres of wild primitive peaks and valleys to be explored.

The South Warner Wilderness lies in the eastern half of Modoc County at the extreme south end of the Warner Mountains.

Seven peaks dominate the South Warner Wilderness and elevations vary from 5,800 feet at Clear Lake to 9,892 feet at Eagle Peak.

A white and pink tower of ash is a prominent feature of the South Warner Wilderness.

The wilderness is surrounded by trailheads, campgrounds, corrals and staging areas that were designed for equestrians. There are more than 80 miles of trails for hikers and equestrians to use.

Devil's Garden

Devil's Garden is an expansive lava flow with sparse vegetation, rough and broken lava rock, juniper trees and sagebrush flats.

While dry most of the time, in the early spring it takes on a more lush appearance as all the water holes fill. It is home to some of the biggest mule deer in California.

Devil's Garden is between Alturas and Canby. Canby marks the spot where the lava flow stopped.

Modoc National Wildlife Refuge

The refuge is south and east of Alturas city limits. It is home to greater sand hill cranes, golden and bald eagles.

In addition to the migratory bird populations, the refuge supports mule deer, pronghorn antelope, bobcats, and coyote.

The Town of "Likely"

A fitting diner for the town of Likely.

This unincorporated town was once named South Fork. The name was changed to conform to the Post Office requirement for one-word names.

One of the last Indian Wars was fought here, and Likely was once the peat moss capital of the U.S. The peat moss was strip-mined from the floor of the Jess Valley and trucked 13 miles to Likely.

Residents were unable to agree on a name until a local rancher observed that they most-likely would never agree on a name. At which point, someone nominated the town of *Likely* and it was voted in.

In 2010, the population of Likely was 63.

Fandango Pass

In 1849, the most-used route to the California goldfields crossed the Nevada desert from Fort Hall into Surprise Valley and over the Fandango Pass.

Because the region remains the same as it was 150 years ago, present-day explorers can walk, bike and ride along the route and relive the emigrant trail experience.

From U.S. Highway 395, six miles south of the Oregon State line, a good gravel road proceeds along the meadows of Fandango Valley and up to Fandango Pass.

For information, call Bureau of Land Management at: (530) 233-4666.

26

Mono County

Mono Basin Museum
And Old Schoolhouse

Old one-room schoolhouse.

The museum is located next to the Upside-Down House. It is filled with artifacts, photographs, books, maps and equipment chronicling the history of Mono Basin.

The museum is located at 129 Mattley Ave., Lee Vining, Ca. Call for information, (760) 647-6461.

Mono Lake

Mono Lake is the largest natural lake completely within the state of California. It was endangered when water was diverted to Los Angeles basin.

The lake's best-known feature is its dramatic tufa towers. Tufa is a variety of limestone, formed by the precipitation of carbonate minerals.

When the water level was higher, freshwater springs flowed into the lake under the surface and reacted with the lake's minerals to form the dramatic cement-like calcium carbonate spires and towers known as tufa.

Mono Lake was formed at least 760,000 years ago. The lack of an outlet causes high levels of salts to accumulate in the lake. The lake is 2.5 times as salty and 80 percent times as alkaline as the ocean.

All year, the Mono Lake Committee, the U.S. Forest Service and the Mono Lake Tufa

State Natural Reserve, lead walking tours and give informative talks.

Mono Basin Bird Chautauqua

We're not sure how it fits this occasion, but we have learned that that the meaning of Chautauqua is either "two moccasins tied together" or "jumping fish".

Twenty-six years ago, birds became a rallying point for the protection of Mono Lake. A Chautauqua is an institution that began in the 19th century to provide higher education opportunities through a combination of lectures, concerts, and public events.

To request a program or register for this event, call (760) 647-6377.

Mono Craters

The Mono Craters are part of a larger structure that includes the Inyo Craters to the south and the volcanoes of Mono Lake to the north.

The Mono Craters are an elongated group of lava domes and cinder cones on the eastern side of the Sierra Nevada.

The last eruption of the Mono Craters took place about 600 years ago

Mono Craters lie just south of Mono Lake and can be viewed from the lake, as well as from Highways 395 and 120.

Bodie Ghost Town

Bodie is a gold rush town in arrested decay.

Bodie is an original mining town from the late 1800s. It now stands in a state of arrested decay.

In 1859, William S. Bodey discovered gold on what is now called Bodie Bluff. A stamp mill was built there and the town began to grow. It started with 20 gold miners and grew to an estimated 10,000 people.

At one time there was an estimated 65 saloons in Bodie.

It's about thirteen miles east of Highway 395, seven miles south of the town of Bridgeport. While it is a less than desirable road, it is worth the trip to see Bodie. Call (760) 647-6445 for more information. Bodie is open all year long.

27

Monterey County

17-Mile Drive

This could be the most scenic drive in all of California. The traveler will experience the wild beauty of northern California's coastline.

Seventeen-Mile Drive goes through Pebble Beach and Pacific Grove, while hugging the Pacific coastline. The drive takes one to the "Lone Cypress" tree and the 5,300 acre Del Monte Forest of Monterey Cypress trees.

The drive serves as the main road through the gated community of Pebble Beach.

The main highway entrance to the 17-Mile Drive is at California State Route 1. There are also entrances at Carmel and in Pacific Grove.

At one time, the City of Monterey and the lands around it were sold at auction to pay a legal bill. David Jacks bought the property for 12 cents per acre.

In 1880, Jacks sold the property to the Pacific Improvement Company, a consortium of

The four railroad barons, Charles Crocker, Mark Hopkins, Collis Huntington, and Leland Stanford.

With the building of the Del Monte Hotel, the area became a tourist destination. Curiously, it was originally called 18-Mile-Drive by hotel operators.

Big Sur

The name "Big Sur" is derived from the original Spanish-language *el sur grande*, meaning "the big south".

Big Sur's Cone Peak is the highest coastal mountain in the contiguous 48 states. It ascends 5,155 feet above sea level and it stands only three miles from the ocean.

The first Europeans to see Big Sur were Spanish mariners led by Juan Cabrillo in 1542. He sailed up the coast without landing.

The Spanish who arrived in 1770 gave Big Sur its name, calling it *el pais grande del sur* (the Big Country of the South).

Archeologists say that Native Americans—the Ohlone, Esselen, and Salinan—inhabited the area. Diseases such as smallpox and measles devastated the Native American population.

Frog Pond Wetland Preserve

Wetlands are considered one of the most biologically productive and ecologically important ecosystems. Wetlands are also one of the most threatened habitats on earth.

Frog Pond retains an important wetland habitat. The 17-acre Frog Pond is composed of a unique arrangement of habitat, including frogs, deer, hummingbirds, towhees, mallards, and western fence lizards.

The preserve offers visitors a great opportunity for nature study, education, recreation and inspiration. The habitat is surrounded by Coast Live Oak, Arroyo Willow and Monterey Pine.

The preserve is located at 650 Canyon Del Rey Blvd., Del Rey Oaks, Ca. Cal: (888) 221-1010.

National Steinbeck Center

The center houses the largest collection of John Steinbeck archives in the United States. There is also a wing dedicated to experiences of agricultural workers, a topic that Steinbeck was passionate about.

The National Steinbeck Center is located at One Main Street, Salinas, California. Call for information (831) 775-4721.

The Boronda Adobe

The Boronda Adobe

The Boronda Adobe was built between 1844 and 1848 in the grasslands of the lower Salinas Valley.

Twenty years later, the city of Salinas was founded and in the 130 years since, the town has grown to within a few hundred yards of the Adobe.

Casa Boronda has the most complete historical record of any residence in Monterey County.

The Boronda Adobe is located at 333 Borona Road, Salinas, Ca. Call (831) 757- 8085.

Monterey County Agricultural And Rural Life Museum

An old iron-wheeled tractor.

Because agriculture is the cornerstone for Monterey County, the Agricultural and Rural Life Museum in King City is an important venue.

Student education is an important part of the Agricultural and Rural Life Museum. In the 2014-2015 school year, 1,832 students toured the museum. The museum held a 4th grade history jamboree with 250 students getting a hands-on agricultural experience.

The museum collects and preserves stories and artifacts of Salinas Valley's agricultural past. It's located in San Lorenzo Park, 1160 Broadway, King City, Ca. Call: (831) 386-0965.

28

Napa County

Old Faithful of California

**Old Faithful of California spews water and
steam 100 feet into the air.**

It is one of three geysers in the world to
bear the "Old Faithful Name" Right on time,
about every 30 minutes, Old Faithful of California spews forth.

Water and steam from an underground river shoot up through a hole in the earth's surface for a spectacular spray that reaches 100 feet above ground.

Native Wappo Indians are said to have seen the waters spew from the ground and used its healing effects to treat tired and aching muscles.

The Indians used the mud from the geyser to treat bee stings and sunburns. Call: (707) 942-6463.

Safari West

You don't have to go to Africa to experience a safari. Right here in Napa Valley visitors can get up close with animals whose origins span the African continent.

Safari goers can travel in an open-air safari vehicle with a guide to explain about the 800-plus animals.

The safari then continues on foot with an exploration of a lower compound and a walk through the aviary.

Safari West is located at 3115 Porter Creek Road, Calistoga, Ca.

For information, call: (707) 379-2551.

Lake Berryessa

Lake Berryessa

Lake Berryessa offers year-round recreation opportunities to visitors. The water reaches 75 degrees during the summer.

Fishermen catch both cold and warm-water species, including rainbow trout, bass, catfish, crappie, and blue gill.

Bird watchers have an array of eagle, hawks, songbirds and wild turkeys. Lake Berryessa's field office is located at 5520 Knoxville Road, Napa, Ca.

For additional information, call: (707) 966-2111.

Bothe-Napa Valley State Park

There's year-round camping, picnicking, hiking, and seasonal swimming at Bothe-Napa Valley State Park.

Overnight visitors will find Bothe-Napa Valley's campsites and yurts. The park has 30 tent spaces/RV sites.

Campsites are equipped with a BBQ grill, picnic table and benches, fire ring, water, nearby bathrooms and showers.

It's located at 3369 St. Helena Highway, St. Helena, Ca. For information, call (707) 942-4575.

Napa Valley Wine Trolley

Here's a chance to have some real fun. Get on the motorized and renovated San Francisco Cable Car and and view the vineyards that produce world class wine.

Pickup is at the Oxbow Market at 610 1st Street, Napa.

You get a gourmet picnic lunch. The trolley makes stops at four family wineries.

For reservations, call: (877) 946-3876.

Napa Valley Wine Train

For those who want a little more elegance with their viewing and dining than a trolley car, take the Napa Valley Wine Train.

The restored antique train takes riders through the Napa wine country to the quaint village of St. Helena.

During the 3-hour trip, guests are served an elegant lunch or dinner. Guests meet in the Oxbow district of downtown Napa.

There are two seating arrangements.

First Seating Section: Enjoy soup or salad followed by your choice of main course on your ride to St. Helena. Then, top off your dining experience with coffee and dessert on your return trip to Napa.

Second Seating Section: You'll be served appetizers on the ride up to St. Helena.. On your return trip, you will dine on soup or salad and then your choice of main course and dessert.

For reservations, call: 1-800-427-4124.

29

Nevada County

Northstar Mine Power House
And the Pelton Wheel Museum

This museum offers hundreds of gold mining artifacts. Visitors will see a working stamp mill and a Cornish pump. The largest Pelton Wheel ever constructed is situated there.

In addition to mining equipment, displays and artifacts, the museum includes a display of articles used by miners and their families in their homes.

It is located at 10933 Allison Ranch Road, Grass Valley, California. Call 530-273-4255.

Firehouse Museum

Nevada City's first firehouse was built in 1861 and is now a museum.

The first display encountered by visitors is that of the Nisenan Indians who inhabited Nevada County for thousands of years. The exhibit includes woven watertight baskets, ceremonial feather dance collars, arrowheads, and pounding stones.

The Chinese played an important role in Nevada County history. The Chinese section displays altars from the Hou Wang and Kuan Yin Temples from Grass Valley's Chinatown 1877-1938.

Malakoff Diggins

The dramatic pit at Malakoff Diggins is true testimony to the devastation caused by hydraulic mining in California.

Malakoff Diggins is where the first environmental law was issued to curtail the release of mud, gravel and debris into major rivers and streams.

Overnight visitors can choose between a shady, restful campsite, or a rustic Miner's Cabin.

Malakoff Diggins is located at 23579 North Bloomfield Road, Nevada City, California. Call (530) 265-2740.

Narrow Gauge Railroad Museum

Visitors can get a docent-led tour of the museum, railyard, and the restoration shop.

The museum collects railroad and aviation artifacts, photographs, and documents for visitors and historians alike.

Collections include the NCNCRR Engine 5, rolling stock, and an early steam automobile.

The museum is located at 5 Kidder Court, Nevada City. Call for information: (530) 470-0902.

30

Orange County

Mission San Juan Capistrano

Mission San Juan Capistrano

The faithful swallows return to Mission San Juan Capistrano each year on March 19. (It's the author's birthday, by the way)

They arrive at dawn and begin building their nests.

Mission San Juan Capistrano is a California landmark and cultural icon. It was founded as the 7th of nine missions established by Father Junipero Serra on November 1, 1776.

The mission's Serra Chapel is the oldest building in California that is still in use.

It is located at 26801 Ortega Highway, San Juan Capistrano. Call (949) 234 1300.

Laguna Coast Wilderness Park

Visitors to Laguna Coast Wilderness Park can see California as it existed for thousands of years. The Coastal sage scrub covers hilltops and slopes, along with patches of native valley grasslands and maritime chaparral.

The park is part of the Natural Community Conservation Planning program. It is designed to protect rare and endangered species, ranging from the California Gnatcatcher to the Orange-throated whiptail.

To learn more about the wilderness area visit Nix Nature Center. Here you can enjoy scavenger hunts for the entire family and learn from free wildlife programs featuring live animals, American Indian customs, craft projects and more.

Nix Nature Center is located at 18751 Laguna Canyon Road, Laguna Beach, California. Call for information (949) 923-2235.

Whale Watching at Dana Point

The warm waters out of Dana Point flourish with sea life, including whales, dolphin, harbor seals and California sea lions.

For fishermen, Dana Point offers private boat chartering for both whale watching fishing. Whale watching from Dana Wharf is free.

Dana Point is located just south of Newport Beach at 34675 Golden Lantern Street. Call (949) 496-5794.

Laguna Art Museum

Laguna Art Museum collects, cares for, and exhibits works of art that were created by California artists or represent the life and history of the state.

Unlike other museums, it collects only California art.

The museum is located at 307 Cliff Dr. Laguna Beach, Ca. Call for information (949) 494-8971.

Knott's Berry Farm

It started as a berry stand in the 1920s and has evolved into a world class theme park.

Here, you can take a stroll down the streets of a Ghost Town, where you may encounter a cowboy shootout.

One of the most memorable experiences at Knott's Berry Farm is the Mrs. Knott's Chicken Dinner Restaurant. It's a fun place to visit and it is handicap accessible.

31

Placer County

The Carnegie Museum

The New Carnegie Library circa 1912.

It's an interesting story behind Roseville's Carnegie Museum. In the 1980s, the Carnegie

Library building was doomed for the wrecking ball.

At a town council meeting, where councilmen were to vote on the destruction, a relative of the McRae family stood up to speak.

She told the council that since they were no longer going to use the land that her family donated for library purposes, she expected to have the land returned.

The original deed verified the Carnegie Library was built upon the land to be used as a library in perpetuity. The original deed was verified and the library was saved.

The 100-year old building became the Carnegie Library Museum.

The library has special collections related to railroads, music and aircraft.

An interesting feature is a railroad crossing gate at the front door which actually swings open for visitors and rings a loud gong to alert staff that someone is coming.

Inside is a room-size model layout of the town of Roseville.

The museum is located at 557 Lincoln Street, Roseville, California. Call 916-773-3003.

Old Town Auburn

While Auburn is one of the oldest towns in California, it wasn't always located in Placer

County. It was originally in the boundaries of Sutter County.

Auburn's new courthouse.

In 1848, court was held in a 20 by 20 wooden building with wooden floors and a zinc roof. The windows held no glass and there were no doors.

In 1851, a legislative act organized the California into counties. Placer County was named and Auburn became the county seat.

On the site where the courthouse stands, bull and bear fights and public hangings were held for the public.

The courthouse that stands there today was built in 1898. The courthouse bell came around

158

Cape Horn and was used to summon officials to court.

The courthouse and museum are located at 101 Maple Street. Call (530) 8889-6500.

The Historic Town of Colfax

As iron rails were being laid up the steep slope of the Sierra on their way to Donner Summit, temporary worker camps were needed.

The Speaker of the House, Schuyler Colfax, was sent by the president to check on the progress of the railroad. His charm and oratory won the people over and they named the settlement after him.

The new town was laid out by Central Pacific Railroad and sold to two merchants, a Mr, Kohn and a Mr. Kind.

Colfax is truly a replica of the old west with boardwalks and stores all with a western façade.

When traveling between Sacramento and Reno it's a wise traveler that will take the Colfax exit. It's like entering a town in the old west.

Denio's Farmer's
Market and Swap Meet

If one can imagine 80 acres of everything in the world in one place it might be Denio's in Roseville. It's open every weekend with vendors coming from far and wide to please the thousands of shoppers looking for bargains.

Surprising antiques may be found among the jumble of merchandise in the wide-spread market area.

It's located at 1551 Vineyard Road, Roseville, Ca. Call (916) 782-2704.

32

Plumas County

The Barn Quilt Trail

The Barn Quilt Trail

Plumas County has joined the Barn Quilt Trail. This started in Ohio in 2001 by a daughter who wanted to honor her mother's Appalachian heritage. Quilt trails have now spread to 48 states ad Canada.

The first barn quilts were installed on some of the most historic barns in the Quincy area. Now more than 100 quilt squares, ranging from 8 x 8 feet down to 2 x 2 foot square, adorn several structures. For information, call: (530) 412-1195.

Volcanic Legacy Scenic Byway All American Road

Chester/Lake Almanor is the southern terminus for this byway, which is considered among the top 20 such scenic drives in the U.S.

This 500-mile byway begins at the southern end of Lake Almanor and proceeds north on both sides of the lake. It continues through Lassen,, stretching all the way to Crater Lake in Oregon.

Views of Lake Almanor and Lassen Peak are the highlights of the trip. There are many opportunities to stop for lunch, shop, take a walk or enjoy a swim or boat trip on the lake.

For more information, call: (530) 487-4583.

Plumas-Eureka State Park

The park gives visitors a glimpse into a fascinating period of California history. The park is focused on building a historical area surrounding it.

The museum was originally constructed as a gold miner's bunkhouse. It now serves as a visitor center.

Outside and across the street from the visitor center is the historic mining area. There is a Mohawk Stamp Mill, a Bushman five-stamp mill, a stable, a miner's residence, and a blacksmith shop.

The park and museum is located at 310 Jonesville Road, Blairsden, Ca.

For information, call: (530) 836-2380 or 1-800-444-7275.

Plumas County Museum

Permanent exhibits include an outstanding collection of Mountain Maidu Indian baskets.

The industrial history wing features railroads of Plumas County, gold mining on the Feather River, and timber.

Outside, visitors can see some of the equipment used by Plumas pioneers. There is a sleigh, a horse-drawn hearse, a water wagon, hydraulic mining monitors, logging equipment, a blacksmith shop and a restored miner's log cabin.

It's located at 500 Jackson Street, Quincy, Ca. For information, call: (530) 283-6320.

33

Riverside County

The March Field Air Museum

There are more than 70 aircraft and more than 30,000 individual artifacts in this museum. March Field has been home to aviation pioneers for nearly 100 years.

These pioneers, some famous and some anonymous, have left a treasure trove of artifacts, from aircraft to flight gear.

Among the aircraft at the air museum are a World War II combat veteran's B-29A Three Feathers" and a B-17G "Starduster".

The museum store has thousands of aircraft related items, from patches, pins, model airplanes to real A2 jackets.

The museum is located at 22550 Van Buren Blvd., Riverside, California. Call: (951) 902-5949,

Mission Inn Museum

Frank Miller, the original owner and developer of the Mission Inn was an avid collector of art from around the world. He was an aviation enthusiast as well.

The Mission Inn is the starting point for a docent-led tour. Located at 3649 Mission Inn Ave. Call (951) 784-0300.

Mount Rubidoux Park

The Peach Bridge on Mt. Rubidoux

There are many different trails up Mount Rubidoux. No matter which way you approach it, there is sure to be a path.

On the summit of Mt. Rubidoux are a number of things to explore.

California Citrus State Park

Entrance to California Citrus State Park

The park preserves some of the rapidly vanishing citrus industry and tells the role of the industry in California's development.

In 1873, two small navel orange trees were sent to Riverside resident Eliza Tibbetts. Those trees grew in near perfect soil and water conditions. Some stories say they were aided by a "dash" of Mrs. Tibbett's dishwater.

The park is located at 9400 Dufferin Ave., Riverside. Call (951) 780-6222.

Botanic Gardens

The University of California's Riverside Botanic Gardens is a non-profit research garden and museum. It is nestled in the foothills of Box Springs Mountains.

The Gardens are a living plant museum with more than 3,500 species from around the world.

It's located on Botanic Gardens Drive, Riverside, California. Call (951) 784-6962.

34

Sacramento County

State Railroad Museum

Old locomotive at California State Railroad Museum

The museum features 21 restored locomotives and cars, dating back to 1862. There is a replica of the 1860s construction site high in the Sierra Nevada.

Visitors will see an elevated bridge, 24-feet above the museum floor.

Excursion trains depart Saturday and Sunday on the hour from 11 a.m. until 4 p.m.

The Railroad Museum is located at 111 "I" Street. Call (916) 445-7387.

Old Sacramento

Both fire and flood ravaged Sacramento during the 1800s before Sacramento's extensive levee system was in place. This brought about the raising of the streets

Today, Old Sacramento Historic District covers the area between the river frontage and Interstate 5.

Gold Rush Days in Old Sacramento (Over Labor Day Weekend) turns back the time to the 1850s. The four-day event is free to the public.

Visitors will see re-enactments of Gold Rush history. There are hands-on arts and crafts for the kids, plus gold panning.

Musicians will play on street corners throughout Old Sacramento. There will be a tent city, showing how miners and their families lived during that period.

Admission is free. For more information, call: (916) 808-7777.

Crocker Art Museum

The Crocker Art Museum is the longest-running art museum in the west. The museum hosts one of the state's premier collections of Californian art.

Among the collection is works from the Gold Rush to the present day.

The museum dates back to 1869 when Edwin B. Crocker and his wife Margaret, assembled a collection of paintings and drawings during an ext5ended trip to Europe.

The museum is located at 216 O Street, Sacramento. For information, call: (916) 400-0017.

California State Capitol Museum

Throughout the west wing and the East Annex, the Capitol Art Program maintains three collected works of paintings. These include the Permanent Collection, the Loan Collection, and the Biennial Senate Contemporary Art Collection.

The combined collection includes hundreds of prized paintings, murals, statues, and antique furniture.

The State Capitol is located at 10th and L streets. Sacramento. For information, call: (916) 324-0333.

American River Bicycle Trail

The American River Bicycle Trail, also known as the Jedediah Smith Memorial Trail, hugs the banks of the American River.

The trail runs for 32 miles between Discovery Park in Old Sacramento and Folsom Lake's southwestern banks at Beal's Point. The two-lane trail is completely paved, with markers, trailside maps, water fountains, restrooms and telephones along the way.

The trail can be accessed from most parks in the American River Parkway.

Sacramento History Museum

See how Sacramento lifted itself up after the floods of the 1860s and 1870s. In 1862, The largest storm California has ever recorded turned the Sacramento Valley into an inland sea.

Ten inches of rain fell in December of 1861. Steamboats were rescuing people from their homes. Governor Leland Stanford was forced to travel to Sacramento by boat for his inauguration.

The Sacramento History Museum tells the complete story of how Sacramento coped with the floods by raising their street levels some six feet.

The museum is located at 101 I street. For information, call: (916) 808-6896.

35

San Benito County

San Juan Bautista Mission

Built in 1797, San Juan Bautista Mission is one of the oldest and largest (It will seat 1,000 people) in California.

The mission was built right on the San Andreas Fault line. Visitors can see an earthquake fault line behind the mission. The 1906 earthquake that devastated San Francisco did relatively little damage to the mission.

San Juan Bautista is an active parish church.

Johnny's Bar and Grill

This saloon is famous for inspiring Marlon Brando's and Lee Marvin's movie, "The Wild One". Johnny's became history on July 4, 1947 when 3,500 motorcyclists rode into this little town that had only five policemen.

They came to rally, race and to party, but never run nearly as amok as "The Wild Ones" movie tells the story.

It's located at 526 San Benito Street, Hollister. Call (831) 637-3683.

Pinnacles National Park

Hike through rare volcanic rock spires, canyons, crags and boulder-covered caves.

The park has 30 miles of scenic trails, a bit of rock climbing and more than 100 varieties of wild flowers, 149 species of birds and 69 species of. butterflies.

If that isn't enough, consider that there are 49 mammals and 400 species of bees and more than 500 species of moths.

Depending on the day, there are often condors soaring over the park area. Condors weigh up to 20 pounds and have a wingspan of nine and a half feet.

The Pinnacles has some of the most unique geology in the world and bears no resemblance to the nearby Gabilan foothills.

Two-thirds of the Pinnacles volcano was split by the San Andreas Fault Zone. The park continues to move northward at the rate of two-thirds of an inch per year.

Hundreds of big boulders like this fall into narrow canyons creating "talus" caves at Pinnacles National Park.

Talus caves are formed by the openings under a jumble of giant boulders which have fallen into steep canyon walls.

Renaissance Faire

Each fall for five weekends, the Northern California Renaissance Faire holds forth at Casa de Fruita. This is sort of all-in-one fruit stand that carries not only fruit but everything else.

During the Renaissance Faire in September and October, Swashbucklers duel for the hands of pretty maidens. Minstrels stroll the crowds, and a costume shop allows visitors to get into the period of their choice.

Casa de Fruita is located at 10031 Pacheco Pass Road, Hollister, CA. For information, call: (408) 842-9316.

36

San Bernardino County

Original McDonald's Museum

Original McDonald's Museum in San Bernardino.

This is a great piece of fast-food history. In 1940, Dick and Mac McDonald opened McDonald's Barbecue Restaurant in San Bernardino, California.

Against the advice of their customers, the brothers closed their successful restaurant, terminated their carhops, and reduced their menu to cheeseburgers, hamburgers, milkshakes and fountain orders.

McDonald's Original Museum is located at 1398 N. E. San Bernardino Street, San Bernardino California. Call (909) 885-6324.

The Fire Lookout Host Program

The first fire lookout was built about 2,000 years ago on Mount Masada, west of the Dead Sea in Israel. It was built by King Herod's army to protect against enemies who were setting fire in Israel.

The first United 'States fire lookout was built in 1876. It was built by the Southern Pacific Railroad on Red Mountain, near Donner Summit.

During World War II, the Aircraft Warning Service was established and the Army Air Force utilized fire lookouts as aircraft observation points.

Fire lookouts are being restored and manned by volunteers. The San Bernardino National Forest and the Southern California

Mountains Foundation report that more than 300 fire lookouts are in use.

For more information on their program call (909) 225-1025.

Mojave National Preserve

The Kelso Depot visitor's center.

The first depot at Kelso was built in 1905.

We're talking 1.6 million acres here. It is the third largest unit in the contiguous United States.

Natural features include the Kelso Dunes, the Marl Mountains, as well as "Hole-in-the-Wall" and the Cinder Cone Lava Beds.

There was a steep grade that trains had to climb west of Kelso to Kessler Summit. "Helper engines" were stationed nearby to help them up the grade.

Steam locomotives needed water. Kelso was perfectly situated to provide both. The first train depot at Kelso opened in 1905.

Norton Air Force Base Museum

This museum is relatively new, having opened in 2013. Everything in the museum has been donated by military and civilian employees at the former base. Norton was closed by the federal government in 1994.

Bob Edwards, a former airman stationed at Norton, Edwards sent out the word, "All the memorabilia that's under the bed, in the closet and in the rafters, what are you going to do with it? "You can't take it with you on your next assignment."

Interior exhibits at the museum include a uniform worn by Kathy La Sauce, the first woman to fly a C-141 jet.

Another display is dedicated to John Levitow, who received the Medal of Honor for saving a plane and its crew during the Vietnam War.

The museum is actively seeking donations of memorabilia to help enhance the museum.

It's located in the former commissioned officer's club, at 1601 3rd Street, San Bernardino. Call: (909) 382-7307.

37

San Diego County

USS Midway Museum

The USS Midway was America's longest-serving aircraft carrier of the 20th century. It served from 1945 to 1992.

"Approximately 200,000 sailors served aboard the carrier, which was known for several naval aviation breakthroughs.

The carrier is now berth in San Diego. Admission includes a guided audio tour, narrated by former Midway sailors to more than 60 locations.

It is berthed at a Navy Pier which has more than 300 parking spaces.

The USS Midway is located at 910 North Harbor Drive, San Diego.

San Diego Zoo

Even if you've visited the San Diego Zoo in the past, you know a repeat visit is always in order.

Their habitats for animals seem to go on and on, no matter if its gorillas, tigers, sun bears, giant tortoises or leopards. Visitors will want to visit the Australian Outback and see the colony of 24 koalas.

You should visit the bamboo habitat and see the giant pandas.

The zoo offers guided tours on a double-decker bus or an aerial view from Skyfari.

The zoo is located at 2920 Zoo Drive, San Diego, California. Call (619) 718-3000.

Del Coronado Hotel

Any trip to San Diego should include a visit to the Del Coronado Hotel, a historic beachfront hotel in the city of Coronado, just across the bay from San Diego.

Del Coronado is the second-largest wooden structure in the United States. The Tillamook Air Museum in Tillamook, Oregon is the largest.

When the hotel opened in 1888, it was the largest resort hotel in the world. It has hosted presidents, royalty, and celebrities throughout the years.

The Hotel Del Coronado is located at 1500 Orange Avenue, Coronado California. Call (619) 435-6611.

Balboa Park Segway Tour

Here's an unusual activity to offer the public. It's a two-hour adventure in Balboa Park exploring the 1,200 acre park on a Segway.

Balboa Park is the nation's largest urban cultural park. It is bigger than New York City's Central Park.

The Segway tours are offered five times daily, seven days a week.

To make a reservation, call: (619) 889-4326.

San Diego Maritime Museum

The Maritime Museum of San Diego has a world-wide reputation for its excellence in restoring, maintaining and operating historic vessels. This includes the world's oldest active ship, Star of India.

Daily public tours are held at 1492 North Harbor Drive, San Diego, Ca. For information, call (619) 234-9153 Ext. 101.

38

San Francisco County

Alcatraz

Alcatraz sits in San Francisco Bay

Alcatraz Prison tours leave every 30 minutes from Pier 33 daily, 8:45 a.m. to 3:50

p.m. Allow at least three hours for the whole trip.

While there are no presentations during the 15-minute boat trip, the views of the city and the bay are spectacular. Once on the island, there are free guided tours.

Golden Gate Park

Some claim that Golden Gate Park is the best city park in the United States, New York's Central Park notwithstanding.

The park has museums, lakes, and gardens. There are biking trails, children's playgrounds and a carousel. Visitors can see buffalo in the buffalo paddocks.

Golden Gate Park was originally part of the largest sand dune system on the west coast.

San Francisco Botanical Garden

The botanical garden covers 55 acres and more than 8,000 varieties of plants. (Tip: admission is free on the second Tuesday of each month, plus Thanksgiving, Christmas and New Year's Day).

Call (415) 831-2090 for details.

Lands End

Lands End is at the city's edge. There developers built the Cliff House where visitors can enjoy ocean views first hand. Spanish explorers named the area "Point Lobos" for the many sea wolves (sea lions).

The area is really an urban wilderness.

San Francisco's Crookedest Street

San Francisco has a lot of very steep streets but it is also well-known for having one of America's crookedest streets.

Lombard Street is so crooked that it is found on many San Francisco tours. Yet there are some who point out that there is another San Francisco street that is more crooked than Lombard Street.

Vermont Street, between 20th and 22nd streets in the Portrero Hill neighborhood is said to claim that honor.

The steep, hilly Lombard Street was created with sharp curves to switchback down the one-way hill past beautiful Victorian homes. Some of San Francisco's most expensive homes are on Lombard Street.

Although the walk is steep, visiting Lombard Street doesn't take a lot of time.

The crooked portion of Lombard Street is located between Jones St. and Hyde St.

39

San Joaquin County

The Haggin Museum

The Haggin Museum is truly worth a visit.

Sunset Magazine called the Haggin Museum one of the "under sung" gems of California.

Its art collection has works of such noted painters as Albert Bierstadt, Rosa Bonheur, and William Adolphe Bouguereau.

The Haggin Museum features exhibits on local and regional history, hosts traveling history and art exhibits.

Every first and third Thursday of the month, the museum hosts with wine and food. On the second Saturday, it has hands-on activities for children 5 to 12.

Located at 1201 N. Pershing Ave. Call: (209) 940-6300.

Stockton Constructed Wetlands

Bird enthusiasts have flocked to the Wetlands at the Stockton Wastewater Treatment Tertiary Facility for birdwatching.

The Stockton Constructed Wetlands was featured as part of the 9th San Joaquin Birding Symposium. The wetlands are becoming an established breeding site for local bird species.

The Audubon Society did a bird count that showed 7,300 birds representing 55 species were present.

For security reasons, bird watching is by appointment only.

The facility is located at 2500 Navy Drive, Stockton. For information, call: (209) 937-8700.

The Stockton Marina

Downtown Stockton Marina

Along the Stockton Channel is the Stockton Marina where a boat owner can tie up right in the heart of downtown.

It's located at the Joan Darrah Promenade featuring beautiful public art.

There are several Delta cruise companies' offering scenic tours of the Delta.

The Delta River Company is offering Delta cruises on its 149-passenger "Princess of Whales". The vessel has two decks.

For cruise information, call: (916) 399-9342.

San Joaquin County Historical Society Museum

The museum has eight exhibit buildings and four historic buildings, including the 1848 Weber House. Charles Weber was the first farmer in the area and the founder of Stockton.

The museum will present the Benjamin Holt story as part of a long-term exhibit on the history of earth-moving equipment.

Benjamin Holt (1849-1920) is credited with perfecting the Caterpillar Tractor. With his brother, Charles, they formed the Stockton Wheel Company.

The first practical field trial of a track-type tractor took place along Mormon Slough near the Holt Manufacturing Company in Stockton.

The museum is located at 11793 N. Micke Grove Road, Lodi, Ca. For information, call: (209) 331-7400.

Cambodian Buddhist Temple

This is an active "Buddhist temple featuring 100 jewel-encrusted statues that celebrate life and the story of the Cambodian Buddha.

Cambodian Buddha

The temple has a 50-foot long recumbent Buddha. The temple hosts an annual Cambodian New Year celebration every April.

40

San Luis Obispo County

Miss San Luis Obispo de Tolosa

Mission San Luis Obispo

San Luis Obispo was the first mission founded in the land of the Chumash people. The neophytes at the mission were called *Obispeno*.

Spanish explorers called the area *La Cana-da de los Osos* (Valley of the Bears). The explorers had seen grizzly bears there.

The mission was built in 1792-94. The mission is located at 782 Monterey Street. Call (805) 781-8214.

Avila Beach

Avila Beach is a hidden paradise on the central coast. There's one road in and one road out. One person said, "Avila Beach is the only place you'll ever visit where you'll never become homesick."

From Highway 101, take Avila Beach Drive exit. Follow Avila Beach Drive for 2.5 miles to Avila Beach.

Bubblegum Alley

Yes, this is indeed a strange sightseeing attraction. But there it stands, right off Higuera in downtown San Luis Obispo between Broad and Garden streets.

It's a narrow alleyway and the site is not for the squeamish who remember finding bubblegum under their desk or seats at school.

Beginning as early as the 1960s in what is thought to be a graduating class ritual or school rivalry, the prank has really stuck.

Bubblegum Alley is a 15-foot high and 70-foot long wall lined with chewing gum left by passersby.

When shop owners complained that the wall was "unsanitary and disgusting" the alley underwent two full cleanings. The bubble gum tradition survived.

Morro Rock

Morro Rock

Morro Rock was formed about 23 million years ago from the plugs of long extinct volcanos. It's been an important navigational aid for mariners for more than 300 years. It rises 576 feet out of the Pacific Ocean.

Portuguese explorer Juan Rodriguez Cabrillo named the rock "El Morro" in 1542. In Spanish "Morro" means crown-shaped hill. It is the last peak of the Nine Sisters, which extends from San Luis Obispo to Morro Bay.

41

San Mateo County

Pigeon Point Lighthouse

Pigeon Point Lighthouse
(Courtesy Gabe Popa)

Perched on a cliff 50-miles south of San Francisco stands the Pigeon Point Lighthouse, It is one of the tallest lighthouses in America.

This lighthouse has been a beacon for mariners since 1872.

The lens itself is 16-feet tall and six feet in diameter. It weighs 2,000 pounds. Guided tours around the lighthouse grounds are available. It's located at 210 Pigeon Point Road, Pescadero, Ca.

Call for information: (650) 879-2120.

San Mateo Japanese Garden

In San Mateo's landmark Central Park is what is said to be one of the finest tea gardens in California. It was designed by landscape architect Nagao Sakurai of the Imperial Palace in Tokyo.

It features a granite pagoda, tea house, koi pond and a bamboo grove. While the tea garden is beautiful throughout the year, it is especially attractive in the spring when the cherry trees are in bloom.

For information call (650) 522-7440.

CuriOdyssey

This is a great place for youngsters. "We treat kids like geniuses," said park spokesperson, Rachel Meyer, executive director.

"We let them loose to observe wild animals, experiment with scientific phenomena and let the natural world answer their questions."

CuriOdyssey has a 60-year legacy but eight years ago, it changed its approach, offering youngster up-close encounters with real science.

It is located at 1651 Coyote Point Drive, San Mateo. Call for information (659) 342-7755.

Pulgas Water Temple

Pulgas Water Temple

It was as a monument to the engineering marvel of Hetch Hetchy Water Project. It brought water more than 160 miles across California from the Sierra Nevada to San Francisco.

It took 24 years to build through the years of the Great Depression at a cost of $102 million. It is located one-half mile south of the Canada Road trailhead. For information, call (650) 652-3209.

42

Santa Barbara County

Santa Barbara County Courthouse

Santa Barbara County Courthouse

The Spanish-style courthouse was called the "grandest Spanish Colonial Revival structure ever built," by architect Charles Willard Moore.

The building replaced a smaller Greek Revival courthouse that was damaged in an earthquake in 1925.

Composed of four buildings, the Spanish-style courthouse includes a jail wing, which is no longer used to hold prisoners. The courthouse occupies an entire city block.

The courthouse is located at 1100 Anacapa Street.

Joe's Café

Joes Café in Santa Barbara

Joe Ferrario, an Italian, immigrant, and his wife, Adelina, bought the Channel Bar in 1928 and Joes Café was born. Joe's Café is the oldest restaurant in Santa Barbara.

Joe retired in 19148 and sold the restaurant to another Joe, Joe Govean. When the second

Joe retired, it was sold to Harry Davis, who made his mark on Joe's Café.

He decided it was too hard to see Joe's Café from the street, so he designed a new and bolder marquee. This landed him in a tussle with the city council. Harry got his way and his sign is still in place.

The present owner is Gene Montesano, who continues the café's legacy.

It's located at 512 State Street, Santa Barbara. Call (805) 966-4638.

Ty Warner Sea Center

The Sea Center is a cooperative venture of the Marine Sanctuary and the Santa Barbara County Museum of Natural History.

Visitors can see a kelp forest in the Santa Barbara Channel and test touch the spines of a sea urchin.

An interactive exhibit allows visitors to sample and test sea water, study animal behavior, and examine microscopic marine life.

You can also see what a tidal pool looks like from underneath through the windows of a huge tank.

The Sea Center is located at 211 Stearns Wharf, Santa Barbara.

Old Mission Santa Barbara

Old Santa Barbara Mission

Mission Santa Barbara was the tenth mission founded by the Spanish Franciscans.

43

Santa Clara County

Ulistac Natural Area

The property was originally inhabited by Ohlone Indians, then by Spanish missionaries. It was later used as pear orchard and then by a golf course.

Now it a Ulistac natural restoration area. It is being restored into a reserve to show the many different habitats in Santa Clara County.

There is an oak woodland, a grassland, a bird sanctuary and a butterfly garden. Call (408) 615-3140.

The Intel Museum

Go behind the scenes in the high-tech world of Silicon Valley. See inside an ultra-clean, highly automatic silicon chip factory.

Visitors will learn about Intel microprocessor history, silicon chip design, and chip fabrication.

The museum is located at 2200 Mission College Blvd., Santa Clara, California.

Call for tours and information (408) 765-5050.

Winchester Mystery House

Winchester Mystery House is an extravagant maze of Victorian craftsmanship. Each step of the Switchback Staircase is just two inches high. The staircase goes up seven flights.

Miles of twisting hallways are even more intriguing by secret passageways in the walls.

Located at 525 S. Winchester Ave. San Jose, Ca. Call (408) 247-2101.

44

Santa Cruz County

Roaring Camp Railroad

Roaring camp & Big Trees Railroad is a three-foot narrow gauge railroad that starts from Felton, California. It runs up steep grades to the top of Bear Mountain.

The steam engines date from the 1890s and are some of the oldest and most authentic narrow gauge steam engines still providing regular passenger service.

Located at 5401 Graham Hill Dr., Felton, California. Call (831) 335-4484

Go to Jail

As a conversation starter, check yourself into jail. Do not pass go, do not collect $200.'

You can do this at the Davenport Jail. It's run by volunteers from the Santa Cruz Museum of Art and History.

The two-cell jail, which opened in 1914, has only had two teen horse thieves locked inside. But don't worry, you can go in and the doors will be left open.

The jail served mostly as a drunk tank. Inside is decked out with photos and displays documenting the history of Santa Cruz.

Bookshop Santa Cruz

Bookshop Santa Cruz has been run by the same family since 1973. An earthquake damaged the brick store building in 1995.

This put the Bookshop annual Birthday Party doubt as there was no building in which to hold it. The staff decided to hold a block party in the street. Everyone was asked to bring five good used books to donate to the Bookshop so it would have funds start over again.

Thousands of people donated books and some brought many more than five books. Others brought their favorite five books, donated them and then bought them right back.

Bookshop Santa Cruz is located at 1520 Pacific Avenue. Call (831) 423-0900.

45

Shasta County

Shasta Lake

Shasta Lake was created with the construction of Shasta Dam across the Sacramento River. It is California's largest manufactured lake.

In 1919, the United States Geological Survey suggested damming the Sacramento River.

Shasta Dam was originally called Kennett Dam after a town that was flooded by the rising waters of Shasta Lake.

When work on the dam slowed because men were leaving for the military, women signed up to work on the dam and it was completed by early 1945.

The McCloud River

The river was originally known as the "McLeod River", after the Hudson's Bay Company hunter and trapper Alexander Roderick McLeod. McLeod explored the river in 1829-1830.

The river rises from the spring-fed streams in the Cascades. It is well-known for a series of waterfalls which tumble over basaltic lava flows.

Cottonwood

Cottonwood was a stagecoach town in 1849. The first post office opened there in 1852. Downtown Cottonwood is a fun place to visit with a western feel.

The town is the host for the California Cowboys Pro Rodeo Association and the annual Mother's Day Rodeo.

Cottonwood is equidistant between Redding and Red Bluff.

46

Sierra County

Big Springs Garden

Big Springs Garden

Big Springs Garden is a summer-only outdoor dining and event facility mixed among a conifer forest and natural springs. It is two miles up the road from the historic mining town of Sierra City, California.

During the summer, Big Springs serves brunch, and on Friday nights in July and August dinner is with live music. The dining area can accommodate 150 people in one setting.

The developed area of the gardens is 30 acres in size. There are cobbled paths, stone bridges and trails with stone staircases.

Call for information, (530) 862-1333.

Kentucky Mine Museum

Historic photograph of Kentucky Mine

The stamp mills are usually silent, but two times a day, they are brought back to life to give visitors a view of an operating gold stamp mill.

A visit to the Kentucky Mine allows families to step into the world of the gold-seeking miners.

:The Kentucky mine is located at 100 Kentucky Mine Road, Sierra City, California. For more information, call (530) 862-1310.

Downieville Museum

The museum is located in a stone building with the original iron doors and window shutters dating back to 1852.

The Downieville Museum has a collection of local artifacts depicting life in the community during the Gold Rush.

Downieville was founded in 1848 by a group of miners who discovered gold there. The town was then named "The Forks".

For a piece of California's great history the drive to Downieville will supply it. Take Highway 49 for about 45 miles from Nevada City. The trip is along the North Fork of the Yuba River with views of the river and forest, both unsullied by human habitation.

There's fishing, hiking, bicycle riding. You can leave your car parked in town while you stroll the easily reachable river on foot. You'll also want to explore the town.

47

Siskiyou County

Siskiyou County Museum

Siskiyou County Museum

The museum was built in 1950. From its humble beginnings the Siskiyou County Museum has grown from a collection of article donated by descendants of early pioneers to a first class history museum.

It is located at 910 South Main Street, Yreka, California. Call for information, (530) 843-3836.

Climb Mt. Shasta

Mt. Shasta

The Mt. Shasta wilderness is an area which for the most part is untrammeled by man.

Each climbing route on Mt. Shasta has a particular season when conditions are optimal. The most popular non-technical route is Avalanche Gulch on the south side of the mountain.

How long will it take to climb Mt. Shasta? The distance from Bunny Flat to the summit is about 5 to 6 miles, depending on the route variation.

For information, call: (530) 926-4511.

Greenhorn Park

Greenhorn Park is the largest park in Yreka and has more than 500 acres surrounding Greenhorn Reservoir. The park is rife with hiking trails, both paved and unpaved through oak woodlands. Dogs on leashes are welcome.

Local legend says the park is named for an Englishman other miners called a "Greenhorn" for his lack of mining skills.

He traveled up the valley where Greenhorn Park is now located. He came back some months later with enough sacks of gold to make him a rich man.

Greenhorn Park has new restrooms, a covered bridge over the spillway, a native plant demonstration garden and an improved irrigation system.

For information, call: (530) 842-5763.

Paul Bunyan's Forest Camp

This camp is modeled after an old-time forest camp similar to what you would have found 199-years ago.

In addition to the Millhouse Museum, the Paul Bunyan Campus consists of outdoor play equipment. The amphitheater hosts a seasonal animal show. The Parrot House is a year-round aviary featuring Lorikeets.

For information, call: 1-800-887-8532.

48

Solano County

Mare Island Heritage Preserve

For 150 years, Mare Island was a federally-owned facility, off-limits to the public. According to legend, the island was once known as Isla Plana.

It got its current name from General Marino Guadalupe Vallejo himself. General Vallejo's animal stock was being moved across San Pablo Bay on a rickety raft when a wind squall capsized the raft.

One of the most-prized passengers on board was a white mare that saved herself by swimming ashore. The mare was discovered later living on the island and gave the island a new name: *Isla de la Yegua* (Island of the Mare).

Il Fiorello Olive Company

Il Fiorello Olive Oil Company

Ann and Mark Sievers produce olive oil from their own certified organic groves on their property in Green Valley and in Suisun Valley.

The name Il Fiorello means "little flower" in Italian. The company is named after Ann's father, Dominic Fiorello.

There is a visitor center for tours and tastings. You can also take a cooking class at the Kitchen in the Grove Culinary Center.

Il Fiorello is located at 2625 Mankas Corner Road, Fairfield, Ca. For information, call: (707) 864-1529.

Jelly Belly Factory

In this tour, the visitor will see a real working factory turning out that candy favorite the Jelly Belly.

It takes seven days to make a Jelly Belly jelly bean. They are made in giant lots in a f actor that shoots out 30 tons of them every weekday.

Tours are free and depart about every 10-20 minutes.

The Jelly Belly factor is located at 1 Jelly Belly Lane, Fairfield, Ca. Call for information, (707) 428-2838.

The Four Museums of Benicia

The Fire Museum

While this museum houses many treasures of fire service equipment, a highlight of the museum is an 1820s double-decker hand-pumper. This piece of equipment required 45 men to operate it.

Guided tours are available by appointment for groups, schools and individuals. For information, call: (707) 745-16883

Benicia Capitol State Park

Benicia was the site of California's State Capitol for 13-months during 1853 and 1854. The town built a capitol building from bricks and architectural materials salvaged from abandoned ships in San Francisco Bay.

This building, with its formidable wite columns, is the historic anchor to the downtown. For information, call: (707) 747-3385.

Fischer-Hanlon House

This residence was once a Gold Rush hotel on First Street. Following a fire in 1856, it was purchased by a Swiss-born Benicia merchant, Joseph Fischer.

He had the building moved to its present location. Here, he added porches, servant's quarters, and privies. The house's Victorian garden is available for weddings and special occasions.

The Camel Barns Museum

The U.S. experimented with camels as pack animals in the 1850s and 1860s. Because of the outbreak of the Civil War, the project was shelved.

Thirty-five of these camels were shipped to the Benicia Arsenal to be sold. The museum houses a variety of exhibits and displays recounting the history of both the City of Benicia and the U.S. Arsenal. For information, call (707) 745-5435.

49

Sonoma County

Safari West

This family-friendly wildlife preserve has more than 700 animals. There are big-ticket African animals, such as cheetahs and giraffes to the quirky little lemurs and graceful flamingos.

The safari is a 3-hour jeep tour. Safari West is located at 3115 Porter Creek Road, Santa Rosa, California. Call for information at (707) 579-2551.

Armstrong Redwoods

Here is an example of what the redwood forest was before logging operations began in the 19th Century. The Armstrong Redwoods are commonly known as the coast redwood.

The coast redwood is the tallest living thing on the planet. The trees live to be 500-1,000 years old and grow to a diameter of 12-16 feet. Some trees stand from 200 to 250 feet tall.

Some coast redwoods survive for more than 2,000 years and tower 350 feet. The rainfall in the Armstrong Redwoods averages 55 inches per year.

The reserve has a visitor center, a large outdoor amphitheater, and self-guided trails. There are picnic facilities.

For information, call: (707) 869-2015.

Jack London's State Park

With more than 29 miles of trails across 1,400 acres, Jack London State Park is part of the allure of Sonoma Valley. The park has a number of historic buildings from the time when writer Jack London called the area his home.

A 2,000-year-old redwood, 14-feet in diameter, stands next to the cottage where London wrote some of his novels.

The Jack London State Park is located at 2400 London Ranch Road, Glen Ellen, Ca. For information, call: (707) 938-5216.

Mission San Francisco Solano

Mission San Francisco de Solano

Fr. Jose Altimira came to California from Barcelona, Spain to manage Mission San Francisco de Asis. Three years later, he decided another mission was needed north of San Francisco Bay.

With help from Governor Luis Arguello, he founded the last of the California missions on July 4, 1823.

Three years later, the neophytes at the mission burned the wooden buildings during an uprising. Fr. Altimira became discouraged and returned to Spain.

Fr. Buenaventura Fortuny, an aging Franciscan, was assigned ro the mission. He quickly restored order. It's located at 114 East Spain St. Sonoma, Ca.

235

50

Stanislaus County

McHenry Museum

McHenry Museum

Rancher-bankere Robert McHenry built this Italianate Victorian house in 1882-83. Most residences in Modesto were built on lots costing $20 to $40 each.

The McHenry ranch, called the Bald Eagle Ranch, was located a distance from town. The dirt road from McHenry's in-town house to the ranch became known as McHenry Avenue, Modesto's main thoroughfare.

Oramil McHenry, Robert's son, inherited the McHenry Mansion.

The mansion is located at 1402 I Street, Modesto, Ca. For information, call: (209) 577-5235.

Gallo Center for the Arts

Gallo Center for the Arts is a performing arts center. The center features two theaters, the 1,200 seat Rogers Theater and the smaller 400-seat Foster Family Theater.

It is located at 10001 Street, Modesto, California. Call (209) 338-5000.

Oakdale Cowboy Museum

The Oakdale Cowboy Museum contains the sights, sounds and smell of the wild west and its people.

Items on display include saddles, buckles, ranching implements, and information on pioneer ranching families.

It's located in the historic Southern Pacific railroad depot, Sierra and East F Street. Call (209) 847-7049.

The Modesto Arch

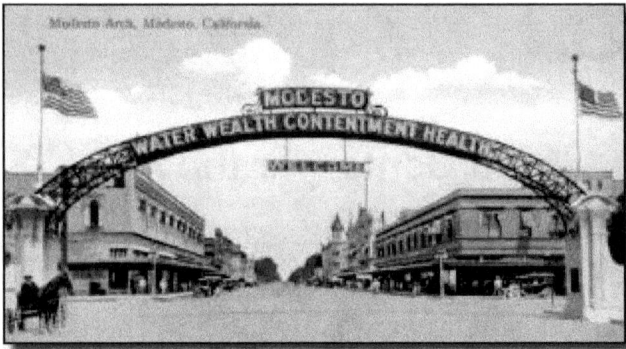

The Modesto Arch

It's been both loved and reviled. The first place choice for a slogan was "Nobody's Got Modesto's Goat". Cooler   heads prevailed and the second place winner was used.

One story claims that Eleanor McClatchy, owner of the *Modesto Bee* newspaper, disliked the arch so much that she banned its picture from being used in the newspaper.

51

Sutter County

The Sutter Buttes

Cat Rock in the Sutter Buttes.

Sutter County is one of the original counties of California. It was created in 1850 at the time of Statehood. Parts of Sutter County were given to Placer County In 1852.

The Buttes are in a circular configuration with a diameter of ten miles. The area covers 75 square miles.

The Sutter Buttes is sometimes called "The Smallest Mountain Range in the World although technically it is not a mountain range,.

The Maidu Indians called the Buttes *Histum Yani,* which translates as "Middle Mountains of the Valley" or "Spirit Mountain."

Community Memorial Museum

The museum is located at 1333 Butte House Road, Yuba City, Ca. Call: (530) 822-7141.

(An interesting side note is that Yuba City is located in Sutter County, not Yuba County)

In 2007, the Community Memorial Museum of Sutter County began work on its long-awaited new Multi-cultural wing. In 2011, the first permanent exhibit completed was t he Japanese-American Community.

Special exhibits in the main hall change every three to four months.

The museum is located at 1333 Butte House Road, Yuba City, Ca. Call: (530)   822-7141.

Yuba City Home and Garden Show

This three-day event is held each year at the Yuba-Sutter Fairgrounds. Promoter Andrew Coolidge manages to attract a host of vendors for his annual show.

(Note: The author will be at this show to sign and sell his several books on California and the gold rush)

Vendors include a wide range of products and services. Visitors will see the newest kitchens and bathroom design, carpeting, concrete brick, and home furnishings.

The Yuba City Home Show is located at the Yuba City Fairgrounds, 442 Franklin Ave., Yuba City, Ca. Check each year for dates as they do vary.

52

Tehama County

Sacramento River Bend

The Sacramento River Bend is a historic and natural resource that presents many recreational and educational opportunities.

The Riverbend offers a diverse habitat for bald eagles, osprey, migratory and song birds, deer and salmon. The Riverbend area is located in Red Bluff.

For information, call the Bureau of Land Management (530) 365-8622. The Bureau's office is at 355 Hemsted Drive, Redding, California.

William B. Ide State Park

William B. Ide Adobe

William B. Ide wrote the proclamation that established the short-lived California Bear Republic in 1846. The new republic only lasted for 22 days.

Ide was a surveyor, a miner, treasurer, district attorney, deputy clerk, and a judge. The park memorializes Ide's role in early California history.

Research shows that Ides never owned the property on which the park is established.

The park is located two miles south of Redding in Red Bluff on Adobe Road. For information, call: (530) 529-8599.

Lassen Volcanic National Park

One of the many falls in the park.

At least four American Indian groups met in the Lassen area. They included Atsugewi, Yana, Yahi, and Maidu.

Mill Creek Falls is the highest waterfall in the park with a drop of 75 feet. It is at the junction of East Sulphur and Bumpass creeks.

Bumpass Hell is the largest area of geo-thermo features in the park. It is in the region once covered by the ancient volcano, Mount Tehama.

Bumpass Hell got its name from a disgruntled explorer Kendall Bumpass, who lost a leg after falling into a boiling pool in 1864.

For information, call: (530) 595-4480.

53

Trinity County

Weaverville

The old west was right at home in Weaverville with its saloons, gunfights and a stagecoach robbery by the notorious Black Bart, who made a practice of robbing only Wells Fargo stages.

An old safe from those wild days is on display in a building now used as a restaurant.

Jake Jackson Museum

The museum focuses on the gold rush days and pioneer life. The grounds contain a reconstructed stamp mill, a miner's cabin, and a blacksmith shop.

It's located at 508 Main street, Weaverville, California. Call (530) 623-5211.

Joss House

The temple is the oldest continuously used Chinese temple in California. On display are art objects, mining tools, and weapons used in the 1854 Tong War.

The temple was built in 1874 as a replacement for another that had burned. It is still a place of worship and provides a fascinating look at the role played by the Chinese immigrants in early California history.

It's located at Highway 299 and Oregon Street. Call (530) 623-5284.

Bowerman Barn

The Bowerman Barn

This barn was built in 1878 by Jacob Bowerman and still stands today as an example of a late 19th century hand-crafted structure.

The Bowerman Barn illustrates the skill and ingenuity shown by people who constructed this building without the benefit of modern tools and techniques.

The barn is located between Covington Mill and Bowerman Boat Ramp.

54

Tulare County

Mooney Grove Park

Mooney Grove Park
In the 1850s, settlers began to occupy
what is now the Visalia area. They found an

extensive forest of valley oak trees growing across the Delta of the Kaweah River.

The towering oak trees covered a large triangular wedge of land. Settlement and agriculture brought many of these trees down. By the end of the 19th century only a few remnant stands remained.

This tract belonged to the Mooney family. After the death of Mr. and Mrs. Mooney, the fate of the oaks looked bleak until a surge of interest rose to save the grove.

The five Mooney children wanted to dispose of the property and invest their inheritance in something more profitable.

A key figure in the "save the grove" effort was John Tuohy, of Tulare. He approached the Mooney heirs and negotiated an option to buy the property. Tuohy wanted to move the oak forest into private ownership.

The park is located at 27000 S. Mooney Blvd., Visalia, Ca. For information, call: (559) 624-7227.

World Ag Expo

World Ag Expo is the world's largest annual agricultural exposition. This three-day event showcases what is new in farm equipment and other agricultural products.

It is held at the International Ag Center in Tulare. Call 559-686-5065.

Tulare Historical Museum

Visitors will learn about the Yokuts Indians, the original inhabitants of Tulare County.

The museum also houses the collection of Bob Mathias, a Tulare athlete who won the Olympic marathon in 1948. It's located at 444 W. Tulare Ave. Call (559) 686-2074.

55

Tuolumne County

The Sugg House

The Sugg House in Sonora

This house was built in 1857 by former slave, William Sugg. He had limited funds and the first stage of the house was built with bricks made of mud and straw.

The roof was made of cut-up five-gallon tin cans.

This structure represents the beginning of Sonora's pioneer period. Sugg came to California with his master in about 1850. In 1854, he purchased his freedom for one dollar.

It's located at 37 Theall Street, Sonora.

Whitewater Rafting on the "T"

The Tuolumne River spills down from the highlands off Yosemite National Park. There are four out-fitters offer one to three day rafting expeditions. The rugged canyon has miles of world class rapids and swimming.

While the rapid run can be made in one day, some people prefer to extend it into 2 or 3 days to explore the river canyon.

Veterans Memorial Hall And Military Museum

The Veterans Memorial Hall and Military Museum is in a building dedicated in 1933 in honor of veterans from Sonora who lost their life. It's located at 9 N. Washington Street, Sonora, Ca. Call: (209) 533-0923)

The Gold Rush town of Columbia

The town of Columbia is located in the heart of California Mother Lode. It is a living gold rush town featuring the largest gold rush era structures in the state.

Folks can visit a working blacksmith shop and watch craftsmen forging finished goods. You can also buy a horseshoe souvenir.

While there, visitors will want to buy a bottle of locally-made Sarsaparilla.

Columbia is located just off of scenic Highway 49. Neighboring gold country towns offer interesting explorations as well. These towns include Sonora, Jamestown and Angels Camp.

Tuolumne County Museum

The Tuolumne County jail was built in 1866 and had become obsolete. At the request of the

Tuolumne County Museum and Historical Society, the jail was designated as museum.

Reproductions of many photos, antiques, and costumed mannequins are on exhibit depicting six geographic regions of the county.

The museum is located at 158 Bradford St., Sonora, Ca. Phone: (209) 532-1317.

Potato Ranch Llama Packers

With more than 26 years of llama packing, we Potato Ranch Llama Packers is the only northern California outfitter renting trained pack llamas.

The llama packers take guests through some of California's best back country, including the John Muir Trail, the Pacific Crest Trail, Emigrant Wilderness, Yosemite National Park and others.

The outfitters are located at 15025 Potato Ranch Road, Sonora. Call: (209) 588-1707.

Railtown 1897 in Jamestown

Railtown 1897 is home to an intact and still functioning steam locomotive repair and maintenance facility.

The center has an authentic roundhouse and shops, and the Depot store is a railroad specialty shop.

It's located three miles south of Jamestown at Sierra Ave. and 9th Street. Call: (209) 984-3953.

56

Ventura County

Ventura Pier and Promenade

This is a pleasant way to see the lively activity taking place in the area. There's a unique space-age playground in the sand west of the pier.

There are vendors selling jewelry and knick-knacks in the pedestrian square.

Walk across the bridge along the tree-lined boardwalk and you'll surfer's point where waves break right beside you.

Olivas Adobe

The Olivas Adobe is the remains of a Mexican Land grant given to Jose Raymundo Olivas in 1842. Raymundo made a fortune selling cattle to the hungry gold miners in 1850.

Raymundo's wife, Dona Teodora, had twenty-one children, who were part of Rancho San Miguel.

57

Yolo County

Heidrick AG History Center

This museum holds a unique collection of tractors and artifacts. The museums artifacts date back to the Gold Rush.

Exhibits show how equipment evolved from the horse-drawn to the steam-driven and f uel-powered   tractors.
Located at 1962 Hays Lane, Woodland, California.

Hot Air Balloon Ride

Hot air balloons are big in Yolo County. Sometime, if you're close enough, you can hear the rush of hot air as the balloons drift higher and higher.

58

Yuba County

Bok Kai Temple

When the Chinese came to Marysville during the Gold Rush, they brought with them their myths, idols, customs and religion.

In 1854, the Chinese in Marysville erected a temple, the Bok Kai Mui, where they could house their gods and go to worship.

They placed several gods in the temple. This is the reason one of the Temple's standards bears in Chinese writing: *Palace of Several Saints.*

Bok Eye is given the most prominent position in the center main altar. Bok Eye is the Chinese god of water and has been called upon in Marysville to prevent floods.

The Bok Kai Festival is held in Marysville annually on the weekend closest to the second day of the month of the Lunar Chinese New Year.

Ellis Lake

Ellis Lake

Ellis Lake has been the most memorable centerpiece of the city of Marysville since the 1930s. It is a sparkling man-made-made lake surrounded by greenery. Ducks and geese have found a real playground here.

The lake is easy to find. It sits between 9th and 14th.

The Feather River

The Feather River's main stem is about 71 miles long. Its length to its most distant head-water is 220 miles.

In 1836, John Marsh, Jose Norriega and a company of me, went on an exploration of Northern California. They felled trees, made dugouts, and ascended the Sacramento River.

As they went up a tributary, they found where the water was covered with feathers. They named it *el rio las plumas*, River of Feathers.

Beale Air Force Base

Tours of Beale Air Force Base are offered on weekdays on approved requests. Tours include specific units such as the 9th Squadron, where technicians discuss and show physiological aspects of high-altitude flight.

Topics may include suit-up of "space suits", decompression sickness, water survival, and altitude chamber training and aircrew ejection from high altitudes.

About the Author

Alton Pryor

Alton Pryor has published fifty-plus books since turning 70 in 1997—many of them about California's past and the colorful characters who rode our trails to fame or infamy.

To date he has sold more than 300,000-plus copies of his first book, "Little Known Tales in California History", and has done respectably well with most of his other titles.

But until fate derailed his 33-year journalism career, he never aspired to write a book, and certainly never anticipated he would come to be regarded as "Mr. Self-Publishing" by his peers in the Sacramento area. "I would have liked living in the Old West," he says. "I wanted, at one time, to be a really good cowboy. I had horses as a young man and even took a raw colt and trained it to work cattle."

But, by the time Pryor was born on March 19, 1927, the era of gunslingers and gold miners was over, and he started life, instead, on his family's farm outside of King City in the Salinas Valley.

He was terminated after writing for 27 years for a magazine. The magazine was sold to a Midwest firm.

Pryor turned to writing books and says now, "I wish I had been fired 20 years earlier."

Index

272

274

275

www.ingramcontent.com/pod-product-compliance
Lightning Source LLC
LaVergne TN
LVHW051458080426
835509LV00017B/1813